POLITICS
KEY CONCEPTS IN PHILOSOPHY

Continuum *Key Concepts in Philosophy*

Key Concepts in Philosophy is a series of concise, accessible and engaging introductions to the core ideas and subjects encountered in the study of philosophy. Specially written to meet the needs of students and those with an interest in, but little prior knowledge of, philosophy, these books open up fascinating, yet sometimes difficult, ideas. The series builds to give a solid grounding in philosophy, and each book is also ideal as a companion to further study.

Key Concepts in Philosophy **available from Continuum:**

Aesthetics, Daniel Herwitz
Epistemology, Christopher Norris
Ethics, Dwight Furrow
Gender, Tina Chanter
Language, José Medina
Law, David Ingram
Logic, Laurence Goldstein, Andrew Brennan,
    Max Deutsch and Joe Y. F. Lau
Mind, Eric Matthews
Religion, Brendan Sweetman
Science, Steven French

POLITICS
KEY CONCEPTS IN PHILOSOPHY

IAIN MACKENZIE

continuum

Continuum International Publishing Group
The Tower Building   80 Maiden Lane
11 York Road   Suite 704
London SE1 7NX   New York, NY 10038

www.continuumbooks.com

British Library Cataloguing-in-Publication Data
A catalogue record for this book is available from the British Library.

ISBN: HB: 978-0-8264-8794-0
       PB: 978-0-8264-8795-7

Library of Congress Cataloging-in-Publication Data
MacKenzie, Iain M.
Politics : key concepts in philosophy / Iain MacKenzie.
p. cm.
Includes bibliographical references
ISBN 978-0-8264-8794-0 (HB)
ISBN 978-0-8264-8795-7 (Pbk)
1. Political science – Philosophy. I. Title.
JA71.M195 2009
320.01 – dc22
2008035397

Typeset by Newgen Imaging Systems Pvt Ltd, Chennai, India
Printed and bound in Great Britain by MPG Books Ltd, Bodmin,
Cornwall

TABLE OF CONTENTS

CONTENTS

ACKNOWLEDGEMENTS

This is a book for all those family members, friends, students and colleagues who have often asked me what I do and who have looked surprised, bewildered, intrigued, amused, and much more, when I say in response: 'political philosophy'. There are far too many of you to list, but this book is really my way of saying 'thank you' to all of you for the many fantastic conversations we have had over the years: at dinner tables, and in bars, coffee houses and seminar rooms. The book is also an open invitation to all to read about political philosophy for yourself in the hope that doing so will encourage you to become a political philosopher as well. As you will see, to become a political philosopher is not just or even primarily about becoming a member of the academic community, it is about exploring political ideas in your everyday life, whatever you do.

My thanks go to the series editors, John Mullarkey and Caroline Williams, and to all at Continuum, especially Sarah Campbell and Tom Crick, for their encouragement, advice and support (as well as their remarkably high levels of patience) as this book slowly took shape.

During the preparation of this book I have had some tremendous expert help, and my heartfelt thanks go out to Anna Cutler, Caleb Sivyer and Martin Larsson for their thoughtful commentaries and constructive criticism. Anna, Kathryn and Sam continue to be my inspiration. What's more, their love and support in helping me to see this project through was beyond any that could reasonably be expected. In the writing of this book, though, Robin Cutler was the wind behind my sails as well as being an astute, insightful and inspiring reader and critic. This book is dedicated to you, Robin.

CHAPTER 1

INTRODUCTION: WHAT IS POLITICS?

In September 2007 Gordon Brown, the then newly appointed British Prime Minister, announced plans to broaden public consultation and to engender a 'new type of politics' (Brown: 2007). He declared that the 'old politics', based on 'a narrow debate between what states do and what markets do', was eroding public services, communities and families. Government, he said, required 'the widest range of talents', a range that should not be limited by party-political divisions. The aim of this new administration, he continued, would be to create a 'politics of common purpose', one that could cross party lines, and therefore engage citizens more firmly at 'the grassroots level'. In the days and weeks that followed this speech, opposition leaders, pundits, party hacks and policy wonks all had their say, and it can be stated without irony that the ensuing debate had a distinctly old-fashioned party-political flavour to it. While there was nothing surprising in this, for those with an interest in politics that stretches beyond simply dissecting the latest pronouncements of 'our leaders' it was notable that Brown's *new* type of politics echoed with themes from the history of Western political thought so loudly that one felt the very meaning of 'new' must surely be at stake. That the talented should rule for the sake of a common purpose, for example, is an idea that has its roots in Plato's *Republic*, written in the fourth century BC; a text generally taken to be the first work of political philosophy in the Western canon. In addition, the theme of broadening and deepening public engagement in political life can be found throughout the civic-republican tradition of political thought; a tradition that can claim roots at least as far back as Roman times. Similarly, the relationship between the state and the (free) market is an issue that has dominated political thinking since the early modern period, not least because their respective historical development seems to indicate what we can call, for the moment, a high degree of co-evolution. John Locke's defence of the natural right to private property, in the second of his *Two Treatises of Government*, and Karl Marx's scathing attacks, throughout his oeuvre, on the alienating effects of private property, are simply two of the more obvious points of reference in this long-standing debate. These examples remind us that thinking about politics is not to be confused with knee-jerk responses to the latest policy announcement. In fact, to think about politics is to become part of a conversation that has been ongoing for over 2,000 years. To take your place within this conversation is to realize that there is so much more to politics than party-political bickering. Finally, to strive to understand what is being said within this conversation, and to contribute to it oneself, is to begin to philosophize about politics. The aim of this book, in these terms, is simple: it is to give you, the reader, confidence to become part of this conversation in political philosophy.

While philosophizing about politics means thinking beyond the everyday to-and-fro of political opinion, it is also true to say that political philosophy must always keep its feet firmly planted on the ground of contemporary issues, movements and debates. In some sense, it is this connection with unfolding events and the desire to understand the constantly shifting sands of our collective life that puts the *politics* into political philosophy. For all that Brown's speech attended (unknowingly?) to perennial problems in political philosophy, it should also be seen as a response to social and political issues that would have perplexed many of the major figures in the history of political ideas. Brown's emphasis on the intrinsic value of community, despite its rich resonance with the writings of classical authors, must also be read as a response to the pressing concerns of the day, such as those that arise from the new phenomena of multiculturalism, climate change and terrorism (to name but three). It is important to remind ourselves, therefore, that although political philosophy is a conversation with the classics, it is also, and must be, a conversation with our own age, our current situation, and our particular political milieu. Knowing this, I think, helps us to feel rather more comfortable with the thought that we may have something to say to our companions in conversation.

This is one way to think about the riches to be found within *contemporary* political thought. Contemporary political philosophers bring new issues to bear on old definitions, put old concepts under the light of new problems, and create new concepts for new problems; as well as much else besides. To give some examples: whether it is John Rawls' creative approach to a theory of justice that must meet the demands of equally reasonable yet different versions of the good life, Michel Foucault's intricate analysis of how networks of power operate across society to 'discipline' and 'normalize' our behaviour, or Judith Butler's groundbreaking work on the social construction of sexual difference, contemporary political philosophy is alive and well and grappling with new ways of thinking about classic problems, with a range of newly identified problems and with innovative theoretical paradigms as well.

Even if we accept that political philosophers must deal with the new every bit as much as the perennial, it may be argued that this is still a very abstract way of thinking about the task of political philosophy. Returning to the classics, for the moment, we can see that while there are those who view political philosophy in a broadly Platonic fashion, seeing philosophy as the bedrock on which politics must be understood and conducted, there are also those of a more Machiavellian impulse who would claim that politics is best considered without the distorting and dangerous distraction of philosophizing about timeless truths and 'imagined republics'. For the 'realist' political philosopher, the task may simply be to provide insight into how political life works, rather than how it ought to be. The Platonic approach to political philosophy, it could be argued, subordinates politics to philosophy; Machiavelli's realism, on the other hand, dethrones philosophy in the name of political pragmatism. Venturing on to a theme that, out of respect for its profoundly complicated implications, I will not seriously consider again in this book, I would caution against viewing the relationship between politics and philosophy as one of hierarchy, whichever term is placed on top. Accepting that political philosophers should indeed inquire into the philosophical nature of politics, we should nonetheless recognize that they must also be concerned with the ways in which political life influences the nature of the philosophical questions we ask. Putting it like this, we can say that to think about the *relationship* between the (allegedly) 'timeless truths of political life' and the 'political life of (what may or may not be) timeless truths' is, in a fundamental sense, *what we do* when we do political philosophy. Political philosophy, in short, is a negotiation between the (often competing) demands to philosophize about political life and to politicize those philosophical claims

3

themselves. It is the to-and-fro of this negotiation that will provide the undertow to the stream of conceptual definitions, debates and thinkers that follow throughout the book; a stream that aims to bring you to the shores of the vast oceans of political philosophy.

WHAT IS POLITICS?

For the purpose of getting started with this tricky question, politics will be treated as a type of human activity, as something we humans do. Certainly, this is already a contestable claim. It may be, for instance, that some of the higher primates also exhibit what we could call political behaviour (de Waal, 1982). It may also be that nature, more generally, has intrinsic value and as such 'makes a claim' on the way we should behave, so that we may have a duty to respect nature – in particular, to ensure its survival – not just for our benefit but because nature itself is worthy of this respect (Naess, 1989). These are important issues, and certainly issues that have spawned a great deal of innovative political philosophy. For the moment, however, they can be put to one side so that we can focus on the human dimension of politics. Besides, once we have a grasp of some of the main humanist assumptions driving political philosophy, we will be in a better position to question and test such assumptions. (There will be elements of this throughout the book as we question, in particular, the idea that there is a definable 'human nature'.)

If we treat it as a human activity, then what kind of activity is politics? In the first instance, we think of politics as something that we do together. Alone, on the oft-imagined desert island, an individual would not be said to be involved in political activity, simply because there is no one to interact with. Politics, it would appear, needs at least two people. That said, not all human interaction is what we would typically think of as political activity (therefore the presence of two people is a *necessary* but not a *sufficient* condition for the presence of political activity). But, just to give a flavour of how prone to divergence political philosophers really are, in putting it like this I am already disagreeing with a formulation by Adrian Leftwich. According to Leftwich, 'politics is a universal and pervasive aspect of human behaviour and may be found wherever two or more human beings are engaged in some collective activity, whether formal or informal, public or private' (2004: 100). I would suggest that the list of other, non-political, forms of collective human activity is potentially quite long, and would certainly include the likes of art, the giving of gifts, love, 'sexual relations' (to use the phrase that Bill Clinton has forever sullied), worship, sport, building, and so on. It is by no means clear, therefore, that two people on some imaginary desert island would *necessarily* be involved in political activity. Nonetheless, if we imagine that they are involved in political activity then we need to ask what kind of interaction it would have to be to constitute *political* interaction. Usually we imagine that politics would arise when the two islanders have to reconcile some clash of interests. It may be that they disagree about how best to distribute the resources of the island, or about how to apportion the island so that each has a part of it they can call their own. When such disagreements arise we would say that the solution to these issues is likely to be the result of activity generally described as political – for example, a debate and discussion about how they should resolve their clash of interests.

We must be careful even with these preliminary remarks, though. We can imagine that there are many different ways of resolving disputes, including violence, trusting to the flip of a coin, or 'divining' a solution from the entrails of an animal. Political activity, it would appear, is a particular way of reaching agreement where disagreement exists and impacts on other people. It implies that those involved – even our two desert islanders – are not just looking to satisfy their immediate interests, but also engaged in a process that aims to establish a set of norms and standards that will help resolve future disputes. This approach to the nature of politics is captured well in a definition by Bernard Crick: 'Politics is the activity by which differing interests within a given unit of rule are conciliated by giving them a share in power in proportion to their importance to the welfare of and survival of the whole community' (1964: 21). Although there is recognition here of the need for the 'welfare' and 'survival' of the 'whole community', it is clear that Crick presupposes that politics occurs where disagreement and conflict occur, and that politics is the art of resolving those conflicts appropriately, that is, without resort to violence or tyranny.

That said, we must be careful of assuming too quickly that politics has the resolution of conflict as its *raison d'être*. Perhaps politics is really a much more cooperative affair, so that political activity is first and foremost a way of binding together groups of people with common interests? Rather than presuppose disagreements and conflict, it may be that politics is best thought of as the pursuit of the common good. Maybe our two desert islanders engage in political activity when they realize that they both place a very high value on liberty, and it was this that brought them to the island in the first place. The political task, then, is not primarily to resolve some disagreement about resources, but to express their shared sense of the good life in as rich and full a way as possible. This is an approach that links a variety of political thinkers, from Aristotle to Jean-Jacques Rousseau and Hannah Arendt. In recent political philosophy, those of a communitarian bent have taken up this notion with the most vigour. In Michael Sandel's (1984) influential article, 'The Procedural Republic and Unencumbered Self', he argues that the liberal individualist presumption that we are beings who disagree about what is ultimately valuable in our collective life, and the legal apparatus that enshrines an individual's right to their own version of the good life, has actually led to a distorted and fragmented political culture, especially in the USA, that is incapable of expressing the deeper bonds that (just about) hold it together. From this perspective, politics is not an activity premised on disagreement, but on cooperation and the pursuit of a good life to which all citizens can ally themselves.

This divide between conflict and cooperation does not exhaust how we think about politics. It must not go unnoticed that these preliminary definitions of politics have been arrived at by way of a contentious thought-experiment. The seemingly straightforward point that politics requires at least two people – either agreeing or disagreeing with each other – was established with the help of a rather abstract example, the desert island. Yet, recalling the opening remarks about the relationship between politics and philosophy, we must be aware of the dangers of relying too heavily on such unrealistic abstractions. For a start, we have glided over the fact that the individuals on the desert island are already political beings. This must be so because we assume that they are able to negotiate their way to an agreement about resources and other priorities: an ability to negotiate that assumes our individuals have a very long list of capacities, attributes, values and concerns already instilled within them, most of which will be embedded in the language they use. Clearly, language is not a neutral carrier of information, but rather it is 'always already' (to use a phrase beloved of postmodern political philosophers) a bearer of political ideas and biases. Our imagined desert islanders are therefore already politicized, even before they begin to negotiate the norms of their interaction, *regardless* of whether it is on the basis of conflict or cooperation. In this sense, then, I would further disagree with

Leftwich when he claims that 'only a Robinson Crusoe-like figure . . . is evacuated from politics' (2004: 100), on the grounds that even Robinson Crusoe had imbibed many political biases and predilections before being shipwrecked on the island. There may be many different kinds of human interaction, of which the political is one variety, but it is also true that we are always already political beings as we engage with each other.

There is no contradiction between these two claims. Not all human interaction is political *per se*, but because we are always already political beings (in so many ways, but especially in respect of the language we use), then everything we do is, in principle, capable of becoming politicized. For example, our two desert islanders may be lucky enough to have a tennis ball wash up on the shores of their home. It seems plausible to argue that they can throw the ball between them in a way that does not constitute political activity. Of course, if one of them throws the ball in such a way that it begins to damage the ball, then they may decide to engage in a political discussion about this precious resource. At which point, the ball-throwing has become a political issue, and they will no doubt draw on their already embedded values and interests in order to secure a resolution to the problem: none of which means that the initial (or even subsequent) ball-throwing should be described as political interaction.

Another concern about the desert-island image of politics can further clarify what is at stake in this fine balance between the universal and the particular nature of political interaction. What image do you have in your head as you picture the desert islanders? I will venture to say that most readers (if you readers are broadly similar to the students I have discussed this with in seminars) will assume that the desert islanders are both male. The pervasiveness of the Robinson Crusoe and Man Friday cultural references explain this, in part. Nonetheless, if we are picturing men, then there is a real danger that a significant set of gendered presuppositions is being built into our allegedly neutral and abstract starting point. This is no trivial matter, since many of the founding abstractions in political thought – most notably the idea of a state of nature (Chapter 2) – are based on a series of biases towards male forms of activity and reasoning (Coole, 1993). Above and beyond the personal biases and preferences embedded in our use of language, for example, there may well be ideas so deeply entrenched in our view of the world that they are part of the *structure* of a given society. Language is clearly one of the principal carriers of such structural aspects of our identity, and it seems true to say that although we use language to express our thoughts about each other and the world (and these may be political thoughts), our thoughts themselves are, to a large extent, already given to us by virtue of the underlying frameworks and structures that shape who we think we are. The desert-island example does little to illuminate this structural dimension to our political interaction. (By the way, are you assuming that our desert islanders are adults? What if they were children? What if Robinson Crusoe was black, or disabled, or transgender? Or all of these and more?)

Indeed, the desire to define politics by way of the desert-island example is an attempt to privilege a certain view of political life: the view that politics is about the interaction of already 'fully formed' (usually rational) individuals. Yet if we consider language and culture, then our views about gender, physicality, sexuality and much more besides must be recognized as already political phenomena, and it is problematic to claim that political interaction is simply that which occurs between individuals. Although politics does happen between people, it would also appear to be going on 'behind the backs' of these individuals. As well as disagreements, therefore, about whether politics is about the resolution of conflict, or about cooperation with regard to shared values, we can now see that politics is also about who we are: are 'we' individual *agents* in control of our own interests, desires, values, customs, and so on, or are 'we' individuals who are profoundly shaped by the way these things are transmitted at the level of social practice and *structure*.

One of the central problems of political philosophy can now be crystallized around these opening remarks. The problem with trying to understand politics is that the definitions one gives of it tend to smuggle in hefty presuppositions that are themselves politically contestable. Or, putting it another way, the way one defines politics tends to have a political dimension to it. Put more strongly, one's definition of politics is necessarily political. As we work through different concepts, theories and thinkers, we shall see how this problem manifests itself. At the outset, though, it is as well to know that when political philosophers disagree about something, they are often disagreeing about how to define politics (even if they don't always say as much).

Are we any clearer with regard to a definition of politics? Possibly not, though we have already gone a long way towards a clearer understanding of one of the core problems in political philosophy. This will be a recurring theme of the book: in political philosophy, we always struggle to find definitive solutions to the questions we ask, but the struggle is (usually) worth the effort in the sense that it forces us (in the end) to ask better questions of ourselves and the political world that we inhabit. That said, whether one prioritizes conflict, and then resolution or cooperation, and then collective resolve, we can see that politics has something to do with the ways in which we are *governed* by *norms*. Moreover, whether these norms are reached through the agreement of more or less rational agents and/or embedded deeply within social structures such as language, politics is a form of human activity that results in, and/or expresses, *norm-governed human interaction*. Political philosophy is the attempt to understand the nature and value of such norm-governed interaction. We will turn to norms later in this introduction. Before that, we can take another step towards better questions about politics if we think through what it means *to govern*.

GOVERNMENT, GOVERNANCE AND GOVERNMENTALIZATION

'To govern' is a verb with many different meanings, depending on the context in which it used. Generally, it means a form of control or influence over a person/people within a territory that guides the behaviour of the person/people within that territory. We might think of the Victorian 'governess' and how she was entrusted with the teaching and discipline of the children under her care within the home.

The term 'government' is similarly broad. It can mean: (a) the activity of governing; (b) the name we give to those who govern us; and (c) a term we use for the apparatus or machinery of the organization vested with the authority to govern. In everyday language use, the context in which the word is deployed separates these different meanings quite straightforwardly. We can distinguish (a) 'the government of the country is entrusted to the Labour Party', (b) 'the Labour Party are the government' and (c) 'the Labour Party are in government'. Although there is a certain virtue in analytical clarity, especially in the fluid and changeable world of politics, I suggest that there is also a lot to be said for retaining this terminological slipperiness with regard to 'government'. However, it is notable that the idea of government, fluid and expansive as it is, does not capture all that is expressed by the idea of politics as norm-governed human interaction.

We can see one instance of this if we consider current trends in liberal democratic politics. Recent years have witnessed the growth of new forms of governance, forms that are not strictly dependent on government activity (although closely related to it). Accepting that the distinction between the state and civil society has become increasingly blurred in contemporary liberal democracies, it is important to explain that a given territory (for example a nation-state, devolved assembly, sub-national region, or supra-national territory) is governed in ways that the word 'government' alone does not really capture. We might think of public-private partnerships, new forms of public sector management with their emphasis on accountability to relatively autonomous quangos, and new forms of policy network that have only a loose connection to the government of the day. Rod Rhodes (1996) has analysed the growing formation of 'self-organizing, inter-organizational networks' that are now integral to governing the country, and he makes the convincing claim that as these networks become more autonomous they resist 'central guidance' from the government. As such, it makes increasing sense to talk of the possibility of 'governance without Government' (1996: 667). Certainly, it is useful to distinguish the formal apparatus of government (and the activity of those who govern over us) from the many ways in which our lives are governed by the establishment of norms that do not necessarily flow from 'central government'. Governance, it would seem, helps us cope with the breadth of the task ahead of us as we try to describe the nature of politics.

Using a longer historical perspective to view the relationship between government and governance, Michel Foucault (1977, 1991, 2004) presents a different picture of governance by contextualizing such phenomena within a much broader and deeper process that, he argues, accompanied the birth of liberal democracies. He refers to this process as 'governmentalization'. Though it may sound clumsy to Anglo-Saxon ears, 'governmentalization' is Foucault's umbrella term for the way the activity of government has been transformed since the birth of modern Western democracies. His claim, in brief, is that the art of government underwent a series of changes in Europe round about the sixteenth century. In late antiquity, government primarily meant the Machiavellian machinations of those in power (the allegiances, power-brokerage, double-dealings and so on) that we generally refer to as forms of 'political reason', or what in French is called *raison d'etat*. With the arrival of modernity and the momentous social transformations that it brought with it, the activity of government became less about internal rivalries and elite treaties, and more about the control of the population. The rise of modern capitalism brought with it rapid population growth and unparalleled movements of people, primarily from the country to the towns. This, according to Foucault, required a new way of thinking about government, a new form of 'governmentality' (from government and mentality). This new form, in essence, became embodied within the set of ideas that we now typically call 'liberal government'. While the traditional narrative that accounts for the rise of liberalism stresses the rights of individuals against the feudal hierarchies, as particularly expressed in the claims of parliaments over monarchies, Foucault argues that the liberal idea of rights was not so much a means to secure freedom, as a means to ensure that individuals do the work of government by governing themselves, so to speak. Liberalism, for Foucault, brought with it the 'governmentalization' of our entire lives so that as individuals we are disciplined into governing ourselves continuously (because the sheer volume of people that must be governed is such that the government cannot simply impose its will on 'the people'). According to Foucault, therefore, liberal regimes are not ones that are defined by the freedoms they enshrine, but rather by the fact that they instil into individuals a sense of freedom which acts as a mechanism for disciplining a disparate populace into governing themselves. Consequently, the traditional apparatus of government is not required for the effective running of a country.

A famous example he gave of this process in action was that of the increasing use of surveillance within society (Foucault, 1977). This is justified in the name of the right to freedom of movement, and the need for security; in reality, though, surveillance makes us all censor our own behaviour in case we are 'caught on camera'. A well-disciplined individual, one who has internalized the need to behave as she or he should behave, is one who does not need heavy-handed government bearing down upon them. While we as individuals think that rights are a means of protection, according to Foucault they are part of a complex social apparatus aimed at disciplining us into 'normal' human activity. On this account, the current government of our own society is occurring not only within the machinery of the state, nor within new institutional spaces carved out since the 1980s.

Rather, we are being governed wherever we are being disciplined into accepting the norms of society: in our schools, universities, hospitals, prisons, homes – and, crucially, by ourselves 'in our own heads'.

It would appear that thinking about the nuances of governing and government have led us back to the concept of the norm, and to the idea that politics is *norm*-governed human interaction. But what is a norm? And how do different answers to this question inform different approaches to the task of political philosophy?

NORMS AND VARIETIES OF POLITICAL PHILOSOPHY

In social and political theory, a norm is a standard of behaviour or appropriate conduct. It is a principle that exerts a certain authority over those to whom it applies so that it serves to regulate their activity. Norms, of course, are everywhere in our personal, social, economic and political lives. Although we are not always conscious of them, we soon become aware of their power to regulate behaviour if we break one. Turning up to work in jeans and a T-shirt on the day of the big finance meeting, in some companies at least, would be seen as a breach of the dress code norm that may even lead to formal warnings and disciplinary action. Where norms are given expression in the legal apparatus of a state, then clearly the consequences of breaking them may be even more severe, even to the point of death. The key concern, therefore, is whether or not the norms that laws are said to embody are morally justifiable (given the possible severity of the consequences, we must have very good reasons for bringing the full weight of the law to bear upon breaches of norms). According to the natural law tradition in political philosophy (including Locke, for example), the norms that should be embedded in our laws are precepts of morality that all rational people would recognize as part of our human nature (which, in Locke for instance, is deemed to emanate from God's gift of freedom, equality and independence to humanity). It is no surprise that political theory and legal theory are disciplines that significantly overlap, because they both give prominence to the norms that govern our behaviour. That said, they are not co-extensive disciplines because the norms that interest political theorists are not only those enshrined in laws (politics therefore being broader in scope than law).

Political theory is often defined as an explicitly normative discipline, its task being to explicate and evaluate the norms governing our interaction. What we call, in short, normative political philosophy is the evaluation of the standards embedded within our norm-governed behaviour, an evaluation that assesses whether or not these are the *right* standards for personal and collective life. It is this view of political philosophy that informs debates about the nature of equality, liberty, justice, sovereignty, and many other core normative concepts. For example, we may hope to base our collective lives on standards that embody our freedom and equality. But, the normative political philosopher asks, what exactly do we mean by this? Are we free when we are left alone, and equal only in terms of having an equal amount of freedom? Or, are we free only when we are in control of our lives in ways that preclude substantial differences in material wealth? Is recognizing a person's cultural heritage a necessary feature of ensuring their equality, or should we treat culture as a contingent backdrop that free beings can, in principle at least, always transcend? Within the contemporary academic environment, it is these kinds of question that occupy mainstream political philosophy. Indeed, for some political philosophers it is only normative evaluation that should really be thought of as political philosophy at all. It will become evident that this is not the view I am adopting in this book, preferring instead to include what we may, with only a hint of a paradox, call 'non-normative philosophical work on norms'; more on this in a moment.

While normative political philosophy has a very close relationship to legal theory, we can also see that (typically) normative political philosophers understand their work as a particular form of endeavour within the broader domain of *moral and ethical* philosophy. Although there are exceptions (notably, Rawls' [1993] revision of the guiding assumptions behind his theory of justice led him to formulate what he called political liberalism, explicitly against the idea that a theory of justice need be based upon a comprehensive moral philosophy), the evaluative demand within normative political philosophy is usually treated as the central task of contemporary work in the discipline. What is right with regard to the norms of social interaction is considered to be a subset of what is the right thing to do, in general. Working within their moral theories, normative political theorists seek to embed justifiable standards of behaviour within institutional designs for government, asking: how should a state be governed in accordance with moral precepts? Can a set of principles be distilled from moral imperatives that can be embodied within political constitutions? What laws should be formulated in order to protect and enhance the moral and ethical principles that are deemed most important? These questions are typical of the concerns that animate the majority of contemporary political philosophy. The most dominant form of normative political theory is liberal justice theory, and within this the dominant figure is John Rawls. It has become something of a cliché to say that the publication of his book *A Theory of Justice* (1971 in America, 1972 in the U.K.) transformed political theory from its hitherto moribund state, and breathed new life into a discipline that had suffered badly at the hands of behaviourist social science. Nonetheless, like most clichés there is more than a grain of truth to it, and this is reflected in the fact that most published normative political theory (almost 40 years later) still takes Rawls' work as a central reference point. For Rawls, 'justice is the first virtue of social institutions'; meaning that whatever else we require of the political institutions that embody our norms of social interaction, they must first and foremost be just. As we will see, for Rawls this means that the norms must be agreed upon by all through a fair process of decision-making where no one has undue power or influence over any other. It is an account of justice that he refers to as 'justice as fairness', because a fair starting point and a fair process will generate norms which are fair for all. We will see later (Chapter 4) how this apparently straightforward claim is developed by Rawls and how it has led to such extensive discussion. For the moment it is enough to recognize that Rawls' approach presupposes that political philosophy is tasked with providing morally justifiable norms that should be embedded within our political institutions and constitutions.

Yet the emphasis on the norms that govern our social interaction does not lead only to the question of whether such norms are morally justified. For many political philosophers, norms must be understood not from a moral point of view but as features of our social life that condition us into acting 'normally'. In other words, a norm is simply a way of imposing on everyone the dominant view of what only some regard as normal behaviour. Put like this, the norms expressed through the social, political and legal frameworks of a country may be techniques of control, first and foremost. Rather than being means to ensure a legitimate political order, they may be primarily a way of ensuring order so that the legitimacy they (allegedly) receive from moral philosophy may simply be a cover for the social order that they maintain.

A question arises: if we allow that this may be the case, then what interests are being served by the maintenance of these norms? A famous answer is provided by the Marxist tradition of political thought: norms are part of a broader ideological framework that distorts reality in the service of underlying economic interests. In the case of contemporary liberal democracies, for example, they serve to distort the reality of people's lives so that the interests of capitalism may be served. For instance, the norms of appearance that seem to dominate today's media serve to support a vast cosmetics industry that makes enormous profits for the shareholders of those companies. From a Marxist perspective, one could argue that cosmetics are sold on the basis of 'beauty', 'self-esteem' and 'empowerment' simply to mask the reality of corporate profiteering behind these pseudo-rationalizations of the industry's legitimacy. Similarly, the legal and political framework of modern liberal states serves to support the interests of capitalism through sustaining the environment in which industries such as cosmetics thrive, and through a myriad of ideological devices that hide the real immiseration of the labourers that capitalists must exploit in order to make profit. As Alex Callinicos (2004) has said: 'Political institutions and struggles arise from, and can only be understood in the light of, the basic conflicts of the social whole. These conflicts are generated at the level of what Marx called the forces and relations of production' (55). On this account, mainstream normative political philosophy not only misses the point (by not focusing on basic economic determinants of political norms), but it is *itself* part of an ideological apparatus that effectively serves to blind us from this (alleged) truth. As Callinicos notes: 'Any study of politics which detaches the apparatuses of state power from their "real foundations" in the forces and relations of production can only offer partial and one-sided insights' (60). The attempt to secure the moral status of norms, and the hierarchical relationship between moral and political philosophy implied by this, is one such partial approach, from this Marxist perspective. In fact, because political disagreement is class-based disagreement and because a post-capitalist social whole would be a classless society, Marxism is described as 'a theory of the abolition of politics' (62).

It may be, however, that the Marxist account is not the best way of thinking about the relationship between norms and ideology. If norms are not ideological distortions of reality, and if ideologies generally are simply constellations of beliefs, then the political construction of norms is simply the ongoing compromise reached by political participants of different ideological persuasions. It may be that *ideologies* (note the plural) are the lenses through which we view the political world – be it liberal, conservative, democratic, republican, Marxist, feminist, or whatever – and it may be that ideologies are relatively permanent features of political life, at least for us moderns. This more neutral concept of ideologies chimes melodiously with our everyday assumptions about party-political activity, where a political party represents an ideological view, each more-or-less legitimate. If we think about ideologies in this way then political philosophy is not about exposing the reality beneath capitalist ideology (note the singular), but neither is it about seeking to find the appropriate moral point of view that will definitively show that one view is superior to others. Rather, the idea of politics as ideological contestation in this sense, according to Michael Freeden (1996), should not be reduced to normative political philosophy because the stress on rigid models of justification and coherence fails to capture the riches to be found in analysing the ideological perspectives of real people engaged in real, sometimes messy and confused, political argument. And, conversely, thinking about political ideologies as the stuff of political philosophy has the benefit, according to Freeden, of allowing us to situate the works of political philosophers within ideological terrains, rather than assuming that the scholarly apparatus and technical language of most political philosophical work simply exempts it from an ideological connection. Freeden's attempt to carve out a space for the study of ideologies as the task of political philosophy is certainly an interesting way of responding to the complexities of political life as norm-governed social interaction, without resorting to the reductionism that often accompanies normative political philosophy or the problematic claims to reality that underpin Marxist theories of ideology. However, it is not clear that Freeden's account considers deeply enough the ways in which the ideological glasses we wear are constructed for us by the underlying social structures that so often condition our experience of the political world. In this sense, it may be an insufficiently critical approach to political philosophy.

A challenging alternative to thinking about the constitution of norms, one that occupies a position between the Marxist and the neutral-analytical, can be elaborated if we return to Foucault. It was noted above that Foucault analysed contemporary liberal democracies as a form of government best understood, not as embodiments of morally justifiable norms, but as a series of institutions that develop techniques of normalization which discipline individuals into 'self-government'. According to Foucault (1977), then, the norm is the tool that coerces individuals into the kind of 'normal' behaviour that enables the government to manage increasingly large and multidimensional populations. The norm is a tool of *normalization*, and for it to be effective it must be secreted throughout the social world:

> The judges of normality are present everywhere. We are in the society of [the] teacher-judge, the doctor-judge, the educator-judge, the social worker-judge; it is on them that the universal reign of the normative is based; and each individual, wherever he may find himself, subjects to it his body, his gestures, his behaviour, his aptitudes, his achievements. (1977: 304)

We can see that, for Foucault, the realm of the political reaches into our bodies. The way we walk, the way we greet someone, and the posture we adopt in a meeting are all the result of nuanced processes of normalization, according to Foucault. In light of this, political philosophy should seek to examine the ways in which these norms are constructed, the limits of the normal, and how transgressing definitions of normality may expose norms of which we were previously unaware. One way of bringing this all together is to say that political philosophy (in this non-normative theorization of the world of norms) is a discipline that aims to politicize the domain of the political.

THE POLITICAL AND POLITICIZATION

Consider this telling passage from Simone de Beauvoir's *The Second Sex*:

> A man would never set out to write a book on the peculiar situation of the human male. But if I wish to define myself, I must first of all say 'I am a woman' . . . the relation of the two sexes is not quite like that of two electrical poles, for man represents both the positive and the neutral, as is indicated by the common use of man to designate human beings in general; whereas woman represents only the negative, defined by limiting criteria, without reciprocity. (1972: 15)

It is this insistence that women define themselves as women first that has blocked their entry into the political world, until very recently in Western liberal democracies (and, from a global perspective, still hardly at all). The diffuse power of patriarchal norms has maintained a firm grip over women's lives for centuries, and prevented them from gaining political access; they have been disbarred from the 'neutral yet male' world of public reason by first having to declare their particularity and emotionality as women. It reminds us that women have had to redefine the very space of the political in order to gain access to it; that what we think of as the political domain must be made the subject of a political critique itself. The political must not be beyond being politicized; that is, redefined. The political world, therefore, cannot simply be restricted to a particular set of issues (security, taxation, and the like) and then left at that: politics involves sometimes momentous redefinitions of what actually counts as a political issue. Women, for example, have had to redefine what is meant by politics in order to gain access to this domain for themselves, and also so that issues pertinent to their lives can be treated as worthy of being included within the realm of norm-governed behaviour. What we think of as 'the political world', in short, has undergone, and will no doubt continue to undergo, transformative moments where previously non-political issues become politicized as individuals and groups expose the effects of power upon their lives.

Feminist interventions in the political world have brought to light the fact that we are often very unaware of the norms that govern our behaviour. To draw an analogy with language, we might say that the political world is littered with 'dead norms' in the way that our everyday language use is littered with 'dead metaphors'. When we talk of the branches of government, for example, we take this as a literal description of the different offices of the state, forgetting that the term implies the metaphorical relation between government and a tree (which then implies additional images about the roots of government, the idea that government is an organism that may be healthy, and so on). Where norms have become dead, we can say that they have been *naturalized*, turned into aspects of our lives that we assume are part of the natural (not the political) world. Perhaps such naturalized norms reveal where power has been exercised most effectively. For example, our commonly held belief that there are only two sexes, and that this is a biological fact, has come under increasing pressure as we have understood that sexual differentiation involves, may even be constituted by, socially constructed gender norms (see Chapter 7). In light of the constant politicization of the naturalized, perhaps the task of political philosophy is to enact the de-naturalization of such phenomena in the name of politicization. Political philosophy, in short, may be the ongoing politicization of the norms that govern our interaction and, importantly, we may not yet even be aware of some (many) of those norms as they hide within our assumptions about what counts as natural and what counts as political.

It is important to be aware, therefore, that what is presented to us as natural, fixed and given may in fact conceal a variety of political issues. This is true of many aspects of life, including the books one reads. This book, for example, presents an overview of the discipline of political philosophy aimed at enticing people into the world of political philosophy, as well as providing a guide to those students who have already found their way into it. As you read it, therefore, you would (rightly) expect to find a relatively dispassionate overview of the academic terrain; and you will. Given, however, that defining politics is a political issue, it follows that providing an overview of political philosophy is also a task that is rich in political decisions and motivations.

The most obvious way of exposing these issues (in any text, not just this one) is to look at who or what is excluded. In this book, for example, there are many fascinating, important and challenging political philosophers, classic and contemporary, who have not found their way into the discussions and debates that follow. From Augustine to Žižek, many have had to be left out. Nonetheless, if this book acts (as I hope it will) as a series of signposts into and within political philosophy, then you will be equipped to interrogate those missing from this text for yourself as you encounter them on your continuing journey into the discipline. But another way of thinking about the political nature of any text is to look at what is included. In this book, there are two areas of political philosophy that I have chosen to highlight as important contributions to the disciplinary conversation: feminism, and poststructuralism. Most other books of this nature barely mention these approaches. My reason for ensuring both of these approaches are well represented throughout is that they tend to operate within *and beyond* the normative mainstream of the discipline and this book is written, in part, to show that political philosophy is broader and deeper than we may imagine. This is a political decision, undoubtedly, and it is not one that you need agree with. I hope, though, that we can talk about the issue, and many others, as we progress through the book, together.

CHAPTER 2

AUTHORITY AND LIBERTY

For Plato, the political world was to be ordered from above. Those with the wisdom and the supreme moral character of philosophers should be the guardians of the ideal republic. Shaping the laws of the Republic, assigning people their proper place in society (even telling the occasional 'noble lie' to maintain order), the philosopher-kings and -queens (Plato was revolutionary in his arguments that women have the same natural capacities for being rulers as men) were seen as the only people capable of creating a form of political association that would be good for all. It was an easy transition for the basic structures of this vision of an ideal republic to become embedded, centuries later, within the emergent Christian forms of political philosophy; philosopher-kings gave way to 'divine' monarchs, and a vision of 'the good life' was replaced with a vision of how God's kingdom could be built on earth. In both views, classical and Christian, political order was to be established from above; through the use of reason by those few who could deploy it fully and wisely, or through the interpretation of God's will by those equipped to interpret it accurately. The claims of morality and of religion were the foundations used to justify hierarchical societies, led by the few whose responsibility it was to maintain order and pursue the good, or God.

At the threshold between antiquity and modernity, Machiavelli's *The Prince* provides us with a third source for the justification of political order: brute force. According to Machiavelli, the princely ruler is entitled to do whatever is necessary to maintain order (given that order is the real *raison d'être* of political life) and therefore can use all necessary means to achieve that end. The people (and, more importantly, the prince's rivals) will not step out of line, knowing that to do so is to risk the cunning and strength of the prince being used against them. A new idea had emerged: it wasn't the claims of morality or religion that founded political order; it was the brute machinations of *realpolitik*. That said, reading Machiavelli's lesser-known but important political tract, *Discourses*, we get a hint of something else, an idea with a long history but one which had until the early modern period been underdeveloped and, consequently, quickly dismissed: namely, that the source of political order may come from below, from the people, and not from above (via morality, religion and brute force). But Machiavelli could never fully commit himself to this new idea; his cyclical view of state development, his cynical view of human nature, his tendency to see dissolution and decay at every turn, his belief in the destructive powers of *fortuna*, and his classically inspired admiration for the great men of *virtù*, all combined to deter Machiavelli from fully embracing the idea that order can come from below.

Furthermore, Machiavelli was a man of the burgeoning Renaissance: the massive social, economic and political upheaval that was to characterize the period of history we call 'modernity' was yet to emerge fully, to seep into the consciousness of those writing about political life. In the 250 years that followed the publication of *The Prince* and *Discourses*, Europe underwent a series of epochal changes, the ripples of which are still dominating how we live in and view the world today. To simplify a rather complicated story: there was the birth of capitalism, leading to an increasingly mobile populace, emergent class divisions, the growth of cities, and an upsurge of new technologies. There was also the rise of modern science, as symbolized by the Copernican revolution, Galileo's challenge to religious authority, Francis Bacon's account of an inductive scientific method, and a whole host of new discoveries about the human and the natural worlds. Moreover, in the realm of ideas there was a subjective turn in philosophy. This was a move away from the philosophical contemplation of ideals towards an internal reflection upon the conditions of our experience that shape what we can and cannot know. This transformation of philosophy was inaugurated by Descartes' method of doubting everything, leading to his claim that the only thing he could be certain of was the activity of doubting itself. This culminated in his famously subject-centred dictum: 'I think therefore I am.'

These developments combined to erode the idea that political order must come from above. People began to question the traditional sources of political order (morality, religion, state force) and, indeed, people began to revolt against and overthrow the established orders that promoted and sustained these forms of political order. As the destruction of traditional sources of order from above left a gap in social and political life all too easily filled by chaos and anarchy, two questions emerged: (a) How could anarchy be avoided? (b) How could political order be established without returning to the discredited traditional sources that had led to the problems in the first place? In short, how could you have social and political order without tyranny? How can order be established, not 'from above' but 'from below'? Put simply, this is the problem at the core of what we now call liberal political philosophy. The concept that liberals often use to straddle the need for order with the requirement that it comes 'from below' is authority. As liberals, we obey the state not because it is rationally founded and morally perfect, not because it embodies the word of God, not because it is likely to use force against us if we do not, but because *we authorize* the state to rule over us and maintain order. But the state is authorized only on condition that it protects our *liberty*, so that we are never again subjected to the tyrannical regimes of feudal Europe. However, as we will see throughout this chapter, getting the balance right between authority and liberty is neither a straightforward nor an uncontested matter.

ABSOLUTE AUTHORITY

The radical idea of securing political order from below had one of its most dramatic, consistent and persuasive renderings in the work of the English political philosopher, Thomas Hobbes – in particular in his magnum opus, *Leviathan*. We can see why the concept of political authority is at the heart of Hobbes' political writings if we consider the context in which he was writing. The political context is clearly stated in the closing pages of *Leviathan*, where Hobbes writes that 'it was occasioned by the disorders of the present time' (1985: 728). These 'disorders' were centred on the rift between king and parliament that led to the English Civil War. His writings, therefore, are deeply concerned with diagnosing the causes of disorder and setting forth a remedy that will bring order (as we will see, this requires the authorization of an absolute sovereign body which we must obey if we are to avoid the terror of living during times of utter chaos). The intellectual context in which Hobbes' ideas emerged can be characterized as one of increasing disillusionment with the scholastic approach to social and political life bequeathed by Aristotle but filtered through medieval Christian thought. Hobbes wanted a more rigorous, less dogmatic approach to the study of political life. He found this in the new science; indeed, he was a friend of Francis Bacon, for a time, and during a trip to the continent he met Galileo. Bacon's systematic approach to the study of nature, and Galileo's revolutionary insight that it was not rest but motion that was the natural state of matter (the law of inertia), both influenced his thought greatly. Indeed, so convinced was he by the work of Bacon and Galileo that Hobbes set himself the task of constructing a social and political theory on the basis of this new method and this new science of motion. Hobbes wrote *Leviathan*, therefore, at a time of profound political crisis, with the aim of exposing the roots of this crisis through the scientific study of the laws of motion that he believed govern human behaviour. Moreover, he sought to demonstrate the truth of his (often unpalatable) conclusions by the careful elaboration of axioms in a scientific and geometric style (Euclid's *Elements of Geometry* was also a great influence on his thought). But how did Hobbes justify the basic axioms on which he was to build his social and political theory? In the 'Introduction' to *Leviathan* we find Hobbes' response to the reader sceptical of how such an axiomatic approach could even get off the ground: 'read thyself . . . [and] he shall thereby read and know, what are the thoughts and passions of all other men' (1985: 82). For all its scientific and mathematical apparatus, therefore, this is still a version of Descartes' inward, reflective and subject-centred approach which inaugurated modern philosophy.

Hobbes' insights into human nature provide the bedrock for understanding his claims about political authority and the nature of liberty. The principle that guides his views is that 'life is but a motion of limbs' (1985: 81). The scientific character of this claim is important: it does not refer to God, or to deeper meanings in life, nor does it make any reference to the direction of life or its culmination. Motion, for Hobbes, is continual motion, and this was his way of bringing Galileo's insight to the most foundational level of political thought. We must not underestimate how revolutionary a claim this was: it was a challenge to the church and to the Aristotelian scholasticism of the medieval intelligentsia, and a broadside against everyday understanding of human nature. Hobbes goes on to identify two kinds of motion: the first is *vital motion*, which begins at birth and ends with death and needs no prior thought (circulation of blood, breathing, or pulse). But there is also *voluntary motion*: this is preceded by an internal motion that Hobbes calls *endeavour*. There are two kinds of endeavour: an *appetite* or desire is when one endeavours to obtain something; an *aversion* is when one endeavours to avoid something. Our sense of being living, thinking beings is largely derived from the movement between the appetites and aversions, a movement Hobbes calls *deliberation*. The last act in deliberation is what Hobbes calls *will*. *Reason* is simply the ability to calculate the likely consequences of our willed action.

Hobbes therefore presents an a-rational, determinist account of human nature: in other words, we are beings that do not have free-will, as our actions are determined by our passions and our capacity to reason is simply the ability to calculate the likely outcomes of our passionately determined actions, rather than a source that motivates our actions. But, interestingly, Hobbes does still believe that humans are free, when freedom is understood 'in the proper sense' (1985: 264). Freedom, for Hobbes, is simply the absence of 'external impediments' (1985: 262). In this way, he can claim that we are *free* so long as we walk down the road without impediment, even though our desire to walk down the road is *determined* by our desire to get to our destination. We are, conversely, not free when someone or something is in the way, and it makes no difference whether it is a natural obstacle or a man-made law preventing our journey. Isaiah Berlin, in his famous essay 'Two concepts of liberty', characterizes this view of liberty as quint-essentially 'negative': 'political liberty, in this sense, is simply the area within which a man can act unobstructed by others' (1969: 122).

Hobbes' real concern, however, is what happens when individuals interact with each other (the words community, culture and tradition must be avoided at this stage, for reasons discussedbelow). In partic-ular, how would people interact if there were no government to rule over them? In political philosophy of this tradition, the condition of being without government is referred to as life in the *state of nature* ('natural' because it is deemed to be life without the *artificial* appara-tus of government). For Hobbes, given that humans are programmed to pursue and satisfy their desires, and that our desires often change, it is rational to obtain what can be used to satisfy our desires, what-ever they are. Individuals in the state of nature, therefore, must secure *power*, where 'the power of a man is his present means to obtain some future apparent good' (1985: 150). But we know that this calcu-lation is open to all in the state of nature. Every individual will want the power to obtain whatever they desire, now and in the future. But we also know that power is relative, which means that the power held by one person depends upon another person not having power. The game of power, in other words, is a zero-sum game: a contest in which one person's loss is equal to another person's gain. The inevitable outcome of human interaction is, therefore, *competition* for power. In contrast to the prevailing attitude of his times, Hobbes did not see any grand harmony in the pursuit of individuals' desires; there is no *summum bonum*, or supreme good, to unite all our individual versions of the good life in one piece of harmonious political architecture. Competition is natural and irremovable from human life.

Is competition such a bad thing? Could competition for power bring a balance or harmony to human interests that would be good for us all? According to Hobbes, two further axioms of human life ensure that competition for power will not bring about a good life. First, humans, like all forms of life, will do all they can to preserve their life; self-preservation is a universal feature of human existence. Second, we must take account of the fact that we are all fundamentally equal. Hobbes means by this that there is no one person who has the physical or intellectual strength to secure power over all of us. As such, we are all fundamentally equal in that we are equally capable of gaining power. On this basis, competition inevitably turns to conflict. Equality means that there is no natural basis for the uneven distribution of power, and the power to satisfy our desires is therefore equally available to everyone. But if conflict is the inevitable outcome of an equal competition for power, then it makes rational sense to try to gain power over someone else before s/he gains power over you. As individuals living in a state of nature, we are forced to conclude that the pre-emptive strike is the rational outcome of such a profoundly conflict-ridden milieu. Moreover, those who are successful (even temporarily) in the pursuit of power will get a taste for it, they will come to know the *glory* associated with power, and they will seek to maximize that glory so as further to secure their power.

So Hobbes sees three sources of conflict in the state of nature: competition for the same resources (but especially power, which by definition is scarce); the fear of the power of others, which Hobbes calls diffidence; and the pursuit of glory as a means to securing what little power one can accrue. If we use the basic axioms of life to construct the natural condition of humanity, the state of nature, then we must conclude that humans will inevitably come into conflict with each other, and that this conflict will take the form of 'a war of all against all'. This is not necessarily 'continual fighting' but, as Hobbes points out, it may be worse, as it involves the continual fear of war. In one of the most famous of all passages from modern political thought, Hobbes describes what life without government, in the state of nature, would be like:

> In such a condition, there is no place for industry; because the fruits thereof is uncertain: and consequently no Culture of the Earth; no navigation, nor use of the commodities that may be imported by sea; no commodious building; no instruments of moving and removing such things as require force; no knowledge of the face of the earth; no account of time; no Arts; no Letters; no Society; and, which is worst of all, continual fear, and danger of violent death; and the life of man, solitary, poor, nasty, brutish and short. (1985: 186)

What do we have in mind when we think about the state of nature? It is tempting to think of it as an historical epoch before the rise of government. Hobbes does mention that 'the savage people in many places of America . . . have no government' (187), implying that they were in a pre-political state of nature which may have been the primitive state of all humanity at one point. However, we now know that such views of 'the savage people' were simply based on hearsay from explorers. More importantly, these views and the idea of a pre-political prehistory are certainly not necessary for the consistency of his argument. More realistically, we can interpret Hobbes as providing us with a vision of what life would be like if government was to dissolve (as it was threatening to do so during the English Civil War). But, to be clear, it is not necessary for us to assume that the conditions of the English Civil War were actually those Hobbes refers to as the state of nature (in fact, they patently were not as terrible as the state of nature he described, no matter how bloody or horrific life during the Civil War actually was). In general, there is no need to think of the state of nature, in Hobbes, as an *actually existing* condition in the past, present or future. Rather, it is better to think of the state of nature as a thought-experiment: what would happen if there were no sovereign power? This is a reading that is consistent with Hobbes' understanding of the basics of the new scientific method – Galileo could not construct a vacuum, but he was able to use a thought-experiment to work out the laws that would apply to a body falling in a vacuum – and it avoids the pitfalls of assuming some fictitious prehistoric and pre-political epoch of human existence.

Nonetheless, how do the individuals in the (hypothetical) state of nature ever manage to escape its horrors? To understand Hobbes' answer we need to grasp what he believes to be the laws that govern human interaction in a state of chaos and war. Hobbes calls these the *laws of nature*. These are *not* moral laws which people ought to obey, as there is no suggestion of good or evil, right or wrong, since everybody first and foremost desires *their own good*. An individual, for example, may desire to kill others (that is 'the good' that they seek power to fulfil), and there is no moral sanction against this in Hobbes' state of nature. So the laws of nature that Hobbes wants to describe are not what his contemporaries would have called *natural laws* (customs and moral ideals common to all 'decent people', regardless of political institutions). The laws of nature are Hobbes' attempt to describe in a scientific fashion (hence the scientific language) the ways in which individuals will reason in the state of nature; that is, it is an argument about how individuals *must* make certain calculations within the extreme conditions of the state of nature.

The most fundamental aspect of human psychology that governs human interaction in the state of nature is that we all fear death. Because there are no moral laws to circumscribe human behaviour (such as that killing others as a form of individual 'good' is permissible), our reason tells us to fear death, and that we must *all* fear death. Clearly, though, we must avoid death if we are to satisfy our desires, so we are forced to the conclusion that self-preservation must be the primary motivation for action. Everything an individual does in the state of nature will be guided at a fundamental level by the logic of self-preservation. This logic inevitably legitimates 'all the helps and advantages of war'; the pre-emptive strike, extreme brutality in pursuit of glory, and so on. But our basic drive for self-preservation also leads us to reason that peace is the best way of providing for the maximization of our desires, as only peace can really guarantee that we will be able to fulfil our desires, as much as is consistent with ensuring peace. This complex balance of forces that get us 'into' and 'out of' the state of nature are summed up in Hobbes' first law of nature: 'That every man ought to endeavour peace as farre as he has hope of attaining it; and when he cannot obtain it that he may seek and use all the helps and advantages of warre' (1985: 190). Of course, it would be irrational to pursue peace if everyone else pursued war. Hobbes tells us that all individuals will inevitably come to realize this, and so there emerges a second law of nature. All humans will pursue peace together. But what is meant by pursuing peace in the state of nature? Hobbes tells us that it means giving up 'the right to all things' and being content with the pursuit of goods that will not impinge on the liberty of others. So the second law of nature is thus:

[T]hat a man be willing when others are so too as farre-forth as for peace and defence of himself he shall think it necessary to lay down his right to all things; and be contented with so much liberty against other men as he would allow against himself. (1985: 190)

Giving up one's right to whatever one desires is only rational when everybody does it, but it is rational for all to pursue this aim because everybody ultimately wants peace so that they can pursue their (now limited) desires more effectively – that is, without constant fear of death. Given that we are motivated in the state of nature to pursue our desires, whatever they are, and that we are driven therefore to seek our self-preservation, and that we have a natural right to use all in our power to secure self-preservation, and given that everybody realizes this, we reason that we must pursue peace by limiting our desires on the basis of equal liberty for everyone.

What is to stop someone from simply ignoring reason, or using reason to secure the submission of others who want peace? In short, this would flout the logic of reasoning in the state of nature because it would immediately place everyone back into the natural condition so that the process of searching for the grounds of peace would have to 'begin again'. This gives rise, according to Hobbes, to a third law of nature: 'men perform their covenants made' (1985: 201). Individuals will necessarily conclude that keeping promises is essential for the pursuit of peace. In a general sense, we can see that reasoning about consequences is what causes the horrors of the state of nature, but it is also the tool which Hobbes' individuals use to extricate themselves from those horrors.

Just before turning to the creation of the absolute sovereign authority, we can sum up three essential claims at the heart of Hobbes' account so far. First, for Hobbes, individuals have only one *natural* right, a natural right being one that is operative in the natural condition (that is, where there is no governmental authority yet established): that is, the right to self-preservation. All other rights are conventional, artificial, 'man-made' by governments. Second, this means that the creation of contracts or covenants is the beginning of justice and injustice; prior to the third law of nature it makes no sense to talk of justice. The breaking of a contract, for Hobbes, is an injustice and 'whatsoever is not unjust is just' (1985: 202). There is no such thing as 'natural justice'; in other words, all justice is 'artificial'. Third, this means that the keeping of contracts demands an authority capable of securing contractual agreements; it is necessary for us to contract with each other to create, to authorize, a power that will ensure that we keep the promises we have made. This authority is created by way of a fundamental, foundational, agreement called *the social contract*.

How is the sovereign power created? Hobbes says it is as if 'every man says to every man': 'I authorise and give up my right of Governing myself, to this man, or assembly of men, on the condition, that thou give up thy right to him, and authorise all his actions in like manner' (1985: 227). The term 'social contract' can be confusing, but we can clarify it in several ways. It is not the mass of individuals in the state of nature who contract with a sovereign body; this is impossible because, by definition, there is no sovereign power in the state of nature. Rather, it is the individuals who contract *with each other* to create a sovereign body. We can say, therefore, that the process of authorization creates an authority; indeed, the individuals in the state of nature are the *authors* who *authorize* the creation of an *authority* which they then obey. Importantly, the right of the newly created authority is the amalgamation of all the rights of the individuals to 'govern themselves'. So the right of the government to govern derives, in this social contract model, from the *alienation* of the rights possessed by individuals in the state of nature; it is because the individuals give up their right to everything in pursuit of peace that the government is endowed with an extensive array of rights. It will only 'give back' those that, in the judgement of government, are not likely to bring about a return to the horrors of the state of nature. To present government as a leviathan, therefore, is to depict it as the 'monstrous' creation of the social contract (a 'leviathan' was a large mythical sea-animal). Government is seen as a monstrous beast, a necessary evil created with the express purpose of securing contracts. This is, therefore, a legal characterization of the state as that which is created to enforce contracts as binding on individual contractors. Enforcing the social contract itself, indeed, is the only way that peace will flourish, and only peace will enable individuals to flourish in pursuit of their (now limited) desires.

There is, though, a notable exception. One right is inalienable: the natural right to self-preservation cannot be given up, precisely because it is not artificial (1985: 192). What Hobbes means by this is not always clear, but I think we can safely assume that it cannot be given up because it expresses what he takes to be a fundamental, irremovable aspect of human psychology: namely, that we will all do everything in our power to preserve our life. Nonetheless, once his position is created by contract, the sovereign has *no* responsibilities to the subjects other than the maintenance of peace through the enforcement of contracts freely entered into. The sovereign authority, therefore, must have *absolute* authority to do whatever is necessary to fulfil this aim; after all, that was the express reason for its creation. The individual citizen has only one natural right, that of self-preservation, all others are to be granted at the discretion of the sovereign authority and, given this, they can be recalled just as easily. This means that 'the people' cannot hold government to account because without the social contract to create the sovereign body there would be no 'people'; only scattered, fearful individuals.

It is worth remembering Hobbes' debt to Euclid's *Elements* at this point. Hobbes liked it so much because it proved unlikely conclusions by deduction from unassailable premises. That we must submit to the will of an absolute sovereign authority because we have given it the authority to rule over us and the only alternative to an absolute authority is the 'worst condition of all', the state of nature, was an unpalatable conclusion to Hobbes' contemporaries (and it remains so to us). The problem is that it smacks of *authoritarianism*, and we will see in the next section how Locke offers an alternative social contract approach that may avoid this authoritarianism. But before we rush to conclude that Hobbes ended up simply defending the absolute power of authoritarian regimes, it is worth considering an alternative reading. We must ask this: on what basis would the sovereign authority pursue authoritarian measures, given that its sole purpose is the enforcement of contracts to maintain peace? If individual citizens in Hobbes' commonwealth are not in the business of breaking contracts, then Hobbes' absolute sovereign will not have much to do: Hobbes' state, in this view, may not be much more than a 'minimal state': 'in cases where the Sovereign hath prescribed no rule, there the subject hath the liberty to do, or forbeare, according to his own discretion' (1985: 271). Looking at it another way also helps to challenge the view that Hobbes defends an overly authoritarian sovereign. Is it not the case that the welfare-democracies that we are familiar with today, while providing help and support to as many of their people as possible, will also, when under threat, rescind the rights of citizens and occasionally resort to the outright use of force against their own members? It could be argued that during the current 'war on terror' superficially liberal and restrained democratic countries are only too willing to override the rights of their citizens if a threat to the state's sovereignty is perceived. So it may be that the real merit of Hobbes' work is that he correctly deduced that all liberal regimes have a thinly veiled cloak of decency to cover up their fundamentally authoritarian nature. If this is the case, then the textbook liberal-authoritarian dichotomy may not exist!

So Hobbes' solution to the core problem of liberal political philosophy – how to create order from below – is this: we must recognize that we have contracted with each other to create the sovereign power to which we must give our obedience, because without this power humanity will dissolve into chaos and anarchy of the most appalling sort. There is nothing in our natural condition, for Hobbes, which will enable us to find order without the establishment of an absolute sovereign authority. On the contrary, absolute liberty will lead to the horrors of the state of nature; we must rest content with whatever liberties the sovereign power we have created gives back to us, and recognize that if we want peace we must have our liberty limited in this way.

LIMITS TO AUTHORITY

The core of liberal political theory was a concept of order from below, without the need for order imposed from above by way of morality, religion or state force: the result is the idea that order from below can be secured if individuals authorize an authority to which they then submit. For Hobbes, this submission must be absolute, because that is the only way of ensuring that there is no collapse into the state of nature. But do Hobbes' ideas stray too close to the dangers of authoritarianism, too close to allowing tyranny in the name of peace and security? Locke, another pivotal figure in the liberal tradition of social contract theory, can be seen as providing an answer to the problem of order from below that nonetheless avoids the (alleged) authoritarianism of Hobbes.

According to Locke, humans must be thought of as free and equal individuals. He says: 'Man being, as has been said, by nature, all free, equal and independent, no one can be put out of this estate, and subjected to the political power of another, without his consent' (1988: 330). Freedom for Locke is enshrined in the ability of individuals to order their actions and dispose of their possessions as they themselves think fit, without needing the permission of anyone else: 'without asking leave, or depending on the will of any other Man' (1988: 269). It is important to note straightaway that this was a direct attack on the ideas of Robert Filmer (author of *Patriarcha*, a famous defence of the divine right of kings). Filmer argued that just as a child is physically and morally dependent upon its father, so humans generally are born as subjects dependent upon kings for their guidance, and kings are divinely ordained as fathers of their country. In contrast, Locke argues that humans acquire their freedom through their possession of *reason*. Reason takes time to develop, undoubtedly, but once the age of reason has been attained, then the individual must be considered free, equal and independent – not subject to the rule of another. Importantly, reason for Locke is not the simple ability to calculate likely outcomes (as it is in Hobbes), but a faculty bequeathed by God to ensure people's good governance of His creation.

So we may be free, equal and independent on account of our capacity for reason, but what are the consequences of this for our interaction? How are we to describe the state of nature, the state before government has come into being, on the basis of this view? A comparison with Hobbes is useful here (though it is important to know that Locke did not write directly against Hobbes). For Hobbes, the passions, rather than reason, motivate our actions. For Hobbes, individuals possess reason, and this enables them to see a way out of the state of nature; but it is the passions, particularly the desire for self-preservation, that are the real driving forces in his construction of a state of nature. Locke, in contrast, emphasizes a person's rational capabilities over their desires. Indeed, quoting Hooker (an earlier writer), Locke sees men as containing only 'defects and imperfections' (1988: 278), hardly the all-consuming passions seen by Hobbes. However, these 'defects' are important, as we shall see later on. Hobbes argues that war and violence are built into the state of nature;

they are inescapable. For Locke this will only happen when the dictates of reason are ignored. If people are motivated by their God-given rationality then their ensuing freedom will not cause conflict. For Hobbes the state of nature is essentially an aggregate of individuals. For Locke the state of nature has a social character, with (as we shall see) social relations functioning in many areas of life. There is none of the same sense of urgency about Locke's account of the state of nature: people are hardly rushing headlong to get out! Locke describes everyone being their own judge, to carry out judicial acts but only in accordance with the law of nature; that is, the law of reason. It is important to be aware of the major difference between the two thinkers suggested by these points; for Hobbes the state of nature was absolutely terrifying, the worst condition people could find themselves in, and therefore the sovereign's power is justified because it provides the best defence against our lapsing into a state of nature. For Locke, the condition of servitude entailed by being under the arbitrary will of a sovereign was far worse than being in a state of nature where (by and large) people acted according to reason, and when they did stray these minor inconveniences would on the whole be dealt with reasonably.

We can see how this divergence impacts upon the two theorists' differing conceptions of rights in the state of nature. For Hobbes the only right present in the state of nature was the right to self-preservation. Locke, in contrast, tries to secure as large an area of natural rights as possible for the state of nature; on his account, if we can see that the state of nature implies a series of rights then any government instituted by the people must respect those rights. One of the most important rights Locke tries to establish is the right to property in the state of nature. Why property? To understand why Locke felt it was so crucial to establish property rights as natural, we can return to his critique of Filmer. As well as defending the divine right of kings, Filmer was a fierce critic of consent theories. One of the examples he used to undermine the idea of consent was property. Filmer argued that a right to property based on consent led to absurd conclusions. A consent-based approach to property, he believed, would mean that since the original state of nature, a state where property is held in common, every act of property acquisition would require the consent of all for the distribution of property to be legitimate. But he thought the 'consent of all' was plainly impossible, and thus the consent-based idea absurd. What was Locke's solution to this problem? First, he asserted that 'though the Earth, and all inferior creatures be common to all men, yet every Man has property in his own person. This no body has any right to but himself' (1988: 287). We have property in our own body, given to us by God, which no person can violate without offence. Second, Locke asserts that 'the labour of his body, and the work of his hands, we may say, are properly his. Whatsoever then he removes out of the state that nature hath provided, and left it in, he has mixed his labour with, and joined to it something that is his own, and thereby makes it his property' (1988: 288). If I own my body, then I own my labour (my labour being what I do with my body), and if I put my labour into something, then the thing becomes mine because I have added my labour to that object, making it different from that which remains in common. If I see a tree and I pick an apple from that tree, then I have exerted my labour and the apple becomes my property. Locke puts it like this:

> He that is nourished by the acorns he picked up under an oak, or the apples he gathered from the trees in the wood, has certainly appropriated them to himself. Nobody can deny but the nourishment is his. I ask then, when did they begin to be his? When he digested? Or when he ate? Or when he boiled? Or when he brought them home? Or when he picked them up? And it is plain, if the first gathering made them not his, nothing else could. That labour put a distinction between them and common. (1988: 288)

Thus, by introducing this idea Locke is able to counter the arguments raised by Filmer. For Locke, private property did not arise from the consent of all, but from the physical contact of humans with the material world. However, it is also worth mentioning that for Locke 'the grass my horse has bit, [and] the turf's my servant has cut' (1988: 289) are deemed to be the property of the person who owns the horse or servant because they are simply viewed as extensions of the labour of the property owner!

Now, Locke himself recognizes a potential problem with this account of a natural right to property. He notes: 'It will perhaps be objected to this, that if gathering the acorns, or other fruits of the earth makes a right to them, then any one may ingross as much as he will' (1988: 290). In other words, given that Locke has made property contingent on mixing one's labour with the material world, what is to stop people from collecting as many acorns and apples as they can find? This idea seems to legitimate the hoarding of wealth, a possibility that would make the state of nature a lot less attractive than it initially seems.

Locke's response is to argue that the laws of nature – and remember, these are equivalent to the laws of reason – actually put a limit on what any one person ought to gather. Reasonable behaviour is to gather only what can be used and enjoyed: to collect so much that the apples begin to spoil and go off before they are eaten is to go against the law of nature, the law of reason; and thus ultimately to offend against God's will. God did not place the lands in common so that they would be spoilt: 'Nothing was made by God for man to spoil or destroy' (1988: 290). The 'enjoyment' of property is defined by 'as much' and 'as good': taking only as much as one can use without it spoiling, leaving the remainder in as good a condition as possible so that others may similarly enjoy the fruits of the earth given by God.

The implication of these moral and religious limits is that in keeping within the bounds of reason 'there could be little room for quarrels or contentions about property'. Locke mentions one other way in which this conflict can be avoided: the use of money. People can gather lots of apples, keep what they need, and sell the remainder so that, having been replaced by money, the surplus apples do not spoil. Moreover, by harvesting and selling the apples, people who do not possess orchards are able to obtain apples. The use of money, according to Locke, is a way of furthering God's will. We can see why C. B. MacPherson (1962) argued that Locke was a pivotal figure in the bourgeois justification of 'possessive individualism'.

It is very important to remember that all the theory so far described refers to the state of nature, which is understood to include social arrangements such as servitude, and also a set of economic relations so highly developed as to constitute a full-blown monetary system. The contrast with Hobbes is obvious. Where life in the state of nature was for Hobbes 'solitary, poor, nasty, brutish and short', Locke's state of nature is not defined by extremities of violence or fear. Indeed, he distinguishes between a 'state of nature' and a 'state of war', saying that the former is 'as far distant' from the latter 'as a state of Peace, Good Will, Mutual Assistance and Preservation and a state of Enmity, Malice, Violence and Mutual destruction are one from another' (1988: 280). But this raises the question: why leave the state of nature at all? What is it that motivates people to contract into a commonwealth? If we remember Locke's account of human nature, we can recall that he viewed the defining characteristic of human beings as their equal capacity for reason. However, it would be implausible to assume that we all follow the dictates of reason all the time; some of us make mistakes, let our passions rule at times, and act without considering the reasonable options. Now given this, and the fact that in the state of nature we are, by definition, all our own judges of what is right and wrong, disputes can arise: the 'inconveniencies' mentioned above. People enter into civil society to avoid these inconveniencies by establishing judges to settle disputes. In particular, government is established so that we have a way of settling disputes about property. As Locke says: '[T]he great and chief end therefore, of men's uniting into commonwealths, and putting themselves under government, is the preservation of their property' (1988: 350–1). Government exists to protect private property, and because our own bodies can be considered property, this includes a commitment to protection of the liberty of individuals.

Turning to the social contract that provides the basis of government, Locke envisages a process whereby each individual agrees with every other to give up to *the people* their right to self-preservation and their authority to judge the laws of nature. Everybody agrees by way of a contract to release this right to the people who from then on become the legitimate judge of right and wrong. While, for Hobbes, the only way out of the state of nature is to give up the right to 'all things' to allow the creation of the sovereign, for Locke the social contract results from the power of each individual being given to the people *in the form* of government. Thus ultimate power resides not in the government itself, but in the people whom the government represents. This is important, because it means that the people become the judge of whether or not a government is acting legitimately:

> Though in a constituted commonwealth, standing upon its own basis, and acting according to its own nature, that is, acting for the preservation of the community, there can be but one supreme power, which is the legislative, to which all the rest are and must be subordinate . . . yet there remains still in the people a supreme power to remove or alter the legislative, when they find the legislative act contrary to the trust reposed in them. (1988: 367)

The legislature is supreme above all other parts of the government (the executive and what he calls the 'federative' or diplomatic function) *but* if the legislature acts against the will of the people then the power vested in the law-making assembly can return to the people. This is why he feels he can justify the supremacy of the legislature and the supremacy of the people: the former is complete under conditions of legitimacy, yet it disappears entirely the moment those in government begin to abuse their power. This general rule has a number of consequences that can be viewed also as specific limits on government action.

For Locke, private property is sacrosanct. Government was set up to avoid the problems involving property ownership, and to protect property, and this was the express reason given by the people for its existence; so it cannot lay claim to people's property; the collectivization of farms, for example, would not be allowed. Inspiring the claims of the American revolutionaries, there must be no taxes without consent. Taxes are an infringement on people's property (which includes their money), so taxes can only be raised by the consent of the people on the grounds that the revenue will be used for the better protection of property. The legislature cannot suddenly transfer its power to another body. It cannot empower the executive to make the decisions; it is the law-making body and must remain so. In general then, the legislature must uphold the good of the community, especially in regard to the preservation of their property.

That said, it is important to realize that Locke was not solely concerned with the limits of government action. He also considered limits on the people, especially regarding their right to rebel. The historical context is worth briefly considering. Filmer had criticized earlier contract-and-consent theorists on the grounds that a government based on consent will not be able to rule effectively. At the first hint of dissatisfaction with the government, he argued, the people will seek its dissolution. This would clearly be detrimental to the effective running of the state and would, in his view, lead to anarchy and disorder. Locke addressed this question by considering whether or not a right to rebellion will 'unhinge and overturn all Polities, and instead of government and order leave nothing but anarchy and confusion' (1988: 401). His response was to place numerous limits on the right of the people to rebel. As the historically sensitive studies of Ashcraft (1987) and Dunn (1969) make clear, Locke was a thinker caught within a complex web of sometimes contradictory political forces, many of which find expression in his political philosophy.

The king's life, for Locke, is sacred, and should be respected, except (and this is a crucial caveat) where the king has declared war on his subjects. In this case the king is effectively placing his people in the state of nature, and the people then have every right to defend themselves, and to attempt to overthrow the monarch. This exception is historically important, because it allowed Locke to endorse the execution of Charles I in 1649. Furthermore, Locke saw it as improper to rebel when the legal means exist to put the fault right. He compares a highwayman who demands £1 from a person at gunpoint to a fraud who steals £100. The highwayman, by using force, has put the victim in the state of nature, and the victim is perfectly entitled to use force to protect his property. The fraudster, however, should not be summarily executed but brought to trial by due legal process, and a judgement passed on him. The same is true of governments that commit illegitimate acts. If they have not acted so as to put people in a state of nature, then they should be ousted by purely legal means. Moreover, if an individual thinks their property has been directly threatened by the government's action, Locke considers it improper for this individual to rebel if the majority are broadly supportive of the government's action. Generally speaking, Locke trusts 'the people'; he trusts that they will not follow unstable leaders, or people complaining unnecessarily or agitating for private gain. This is reflected in another limit on rebellion, but a slightly different one. Locke believes the majority must only rebel when they are seriously aggrieved, by which he means that long-term injustice has been inflicted upon them. The majority, even if they are angry, should not rebel for trivial reasons; they must have good cause – and time is a measure of good cause.

The important aspect of the last two limits on rebellion is that Locke equates the will of the majority with what is right. If 'the people' decide that a government has acted either legitimately or illegitimately, the people are right. This is very problematical for many political philosophers. Two centuries after Locke, and therefore long after the first flush of bourgeois liberal revolutions against feudal powers, John Stuart Mill, a liberal of Victorian ilk, argued that the people were not always right, and that to assume so could have serious consequences for individual liberty.

INDIVIDUAL LIBERTY

Mill was deeply influenced by Alexis de Tocqueville's critique of the standardization of life in democratic America, and the lack of independence of thought it allowed its citizens: 'I know of no country,' said de Tocqueville, 'in which, speaking generally, there is less independence of mind and true freedom of discussion than in America' (1966: 254–5). Mill was persuaded that the consequence of this loss of independence was, as de Tocqueville claimed, the 'tyranny of the majority'. From this analysis, Mill constructed a very useful rejoinder to those liberals, like Locke, who relied too readily on a politics of 'trust in the people'. Mill agreed that a democratic political system could lead to the kind of conformity that might stifle free thinking. Even where the formal system of government created the conditions for freedom to flourish, the informal power wielded by majorities was often 'more formidable than many kinds of political oppression . . . it leaves fewer means of escape, penetrating much more deeply into the details of life and enslaving the soul itself' (1972: 73). This is because, as Mill notes, 'where society is itself the tyrant – society collectively over the separate individuals who compose it – its means of tyrannizing are not restricted to the acts which it may do by the hands of its political functionaries' (1972: 73). This reveals that the free thought of individuals is of paramount importance to Mill; for him, freedom of thought is the only way of ensuring that society as a whole moves closer to the truth:

> If the opinion is right, they [the majority] are deprived of the opportunity of exchanging error for truth; if wrong, they lose, what is almost as great a benefit, the clearer perception and livelier impression of truth, produced by its collision with error. (1972: 85)

This view, though at odds with Locke's liberal trust in the people, has become a cornerstone of liberal ideology. Commonly presented as the saying 'I may not agree with what you say but I defend your right to say it' (usually misattributed to Voltaire), liberty of conscience and expression have become bulwarks against the tendency of prejudiced majorities in liberal democratic authorities towards mediocrity and oppression. But how is freedom of opinion to be enshrined? Tackling this issue, Mill develops his 'one very simple principle', the liberty principle:

> [T]he sole end for which mankind are warranted, individually or collectively, in interfering with the liberty of action of any of their number, is self-protection. That the only purpose for which power

can be rightfully exercised over any member of a civilized community, against his will, is to prevent harm to others. (1972: 78)

Also known as 'the harm principle', Mill's definition of personal freedom seems straightforward. Indeed, it would appear that this 'simple principle' would legitimate a very large degree of personal freedom. Applying it in contemporary terms, it could lead to the rejection of laws prohibiting many activities that may not cause harm to other people: the use of pornography, the taking of drugs, sado-masochistic sexual activities, and much else besides. In this sense, Mill's liberty principle could, as Mill intended, be used as the basis for promoting 'experiments in living' by giving the 'freest scope possible to uncustomary things' (1972: 135). Encouraging individuals to move beyond conventional ways of life can be seen as a useful corrective to placing too much trust in a majority population that tends toward the 'despotism of custom'. Of course, the 'liberty principle' could be said to move too far in the opposite direction, allowing chaotic experimentalism to take the place of an ordered life. Mill was careful to avoid such implications and we shall see (in Chapter 4) how his advocacy of representative government actually places a significant burden of public duty on individuals to take part in the life of democratic institutions.

Nonetheless, Mill's one simple principle is notoriously fraught with problems, most obviously relating to the concept of 'harm'. For instance, how do we define harm? If one is engaged in what Mill calls 'a purely self-regarding action' such as drinking alcohol, then is it true to say that, to the extent that it might affect others at all, it only affects them 'indirectly' and therefore causes no 'direct' harm that would warrant the individual being stopped from drinking? It may be possible to maintain the idea of 'direct harm' if, as with Mill, one defines harm as physical harm. Is this enough, however, to secure the liberty principle? It could be suggested that much of what counts as harm, and would therefore violate of a person's freedom, has a 'psychological' dimension to it. Furthermore, Mill argues that intervention in other people's lives is not justified if it is being done for the 'good' of those other people. Yet, as we shall see in the discussion of Rousseau that follows, it may be that 'forcing people to be free' is just what is required to make them free. Looking further ahead, we shall see in Chapter 3 that according to Catharine MacKinnon, defining the harm that women suffer through pornography may not be limited to those who work in the pornography industry. It may be, as MacKinnon argues, that pornography plays its part in structural rather than individual harm against women. In other words, as we consider the implications of Mill's 'one simple principle', we see a need for a whole host of carefully placed qualifiers, playing essential roles by preventing harm in particular areas of unassailable personal freedom. Maybe the real task is not to set liberty against the overbearing state, but to find a way of combining our freedom with the authority we vest in the state. This is the approach we find in the work of Jean-Jacques Rousseau.

LIBERTY AND THE GENERAL WILL

In Hobbes we saw how the demands of creating a stable authority may have led to the institution of political authoritarianism. Locke's version of the social contract sought to prevent this problem by investing the ultimate authority in the community; the community then authorizes government to carry out its wishes, but if it fails to do so then the community has the right, under specific circumstances, to revolt against the government. For both Hobbes and Locke, the state of nature is a device to explain how individuals could give up their rights, to the sovereign and to the people respectively. For Hobbes, the primary end of government is peace and security, because the government exists to prevent a collapse into the state of nature. So, with security established, we can pursue our desires as fully as possible, within the limits of liberty – that is, as long as we don't prevent anyone else from pursuing their desires. For Locke, the government exists to protect private property, and government is entrusted by the people to adjudicate on disputes about property.

Hobbes saw absolute authority as the guarantor of peace amongst individuals naturally predisposed towards conflict, and Locke saw that government must be limited in order to protect the property rights and liberties of individuals against abuses of power by the government; but there is still a tension between authority and liberty. If the people and the government 'spoke with one voice', and if there was no conflict between the individual good and the collective good, would the problem of authority have reached a rational and final solution? Rather than see authority as the glue that sticks individuals together into collectives, by way of government, should we not think of governmental authority as expressive of that which is good for us all, in a much wider sense than simply preserving the peace or protecting our property? Moreover, is it not the case that private property, competitive individualism and social conflict are symptoms of a system that has gone wrong, rather than a natural outcome of the interaction of people with each other and the natural world? If so, why should we seek to build governmental authority on symptoms of social decline which ultimately prevent us from realizing our sense of a truly harmonious and collective good life? Did Hobbes and Locke start with the wrong assumptions, and therefore articulate a truncated or impoverished concept of political authority? It is these, and related questions, that lead us to the work of Jean-Jacques Rousseau; in particular, his essay 'A discourse on the origin of inequality' and his book, *The Social Contract.*

While it is possible to see Rousseau as a radical thinker (this was the view of the French revolutionaries who exhumed his body and placed it in the Pantheon), this is only a small part of a much more complex picture. Rousseau was certainly a philosopher associated with the major figures of the French Enlightenment, such as Diderot (though by all accounts their relationship was fraught), but his major themes and preoccupations were not straightforwardly derived from an Enlightenment perspective on the world. In particular, Rousseau was one of the first great critics of the ongoing processes of civilization and human cultivation that so many Enlightenment thinkers took as a sign of 'man's' new-found triumph of reason over emotion and over nature. Indeed, Rousseau saw that too much reason (of a certain variety) led to a shrinking of our natural sympathy towards others and also to weakness on the battlefield, where virtues other than reasonableness were paramount. So, is there anything to link Rousseau's arguments for a new rational form of authority in which the will of all is harmonious with the will of each individual, with his critique of the role of reason in enslaving and impoverishing humanity by detaching us from ourselves? In a word, freedom; in three words, freedom from dependency; and in another word, autonomy. Without neglecting the internal inconsistencies present in Rousseau's work, we can unify his critique of social and political institutions and his call for a new social contract by thinking in terms of what it means to be free. Immediately, it is worth noting that Rousseau's understanding of liberty differs markedly from the accounts of 'negative freedom' – to use the concept developed by Berlin (1969) – which are found in Hobbes and Locke. Rousseau develops a 'positive' account of human freedom which Berlin has defined as 'the freedom which consists in being one's own master' (1969: 131). For Rousseau, liberty and authority will finally reach a harmonious unity when humanity establishes a 'form of association which will defend and protect with the whole common force the person and the goods of each associate and in which each, whilst uniting himself with all, may still obey himself alone and be as free as before' (1973: 174). The problem of establishing such a polity, he claims, is one to which the social contract provides the solution. Rousseau is therefore a social-contract political philosopher and he uses the concepts and devices which social contract theory bequeaths: the state of nature, the social contract itself, and the legitimate authority it creates. We can look at each in turn to see how Rousseau argues that we can reconcile the demand for authority and liberty with the notion of the general will.

In some respects, Rousseau's vision of the state of nature takes us back to Hobbes: where Locke had envisioned an array of social institutions in the state of nature and wrapped these up in theologically derived moral/natural laws, Rousseau's vision is of isolated individuals wandering the forests, satisfying their desires as and when they please, with no social apparatus apparent and no moral laws operative. Of course, Hobbes and Rousseau differ on what the outcome of this natural condition will be. For Hobbes, individuals left to their own devices without a sovereign body to rule over them will inevitably descend into warfare and conflict. For Rousseau, individuals in a natural condition will live a life in pursuit of their own survival; but there is nothing to suggest that this will cause conflict, at least of the systemic kind that Hobbes envisioned. After all, claims Rousseau, animals do not live in a condition of systematic conflict, for all that they fight. Rousseau argued that Hobbes had in fact described the characteristics of '*social* man' in his account of the allegedly natural condition of humanity. This was true of all those other philosophers who used the idea of a state of nature:

> The philosophers, who have inquired into the foundations of society, have all felt the necessity of going back to a state of nature; but not one of them has got there . . . Every one of them, in short, constantly dwelling on wants, avidity, oppression, desires and pride has transferred to the state of nature ideas that were acquired in society; so that, in speaking of the savage, they described the social man. (1973: 45)

Rousseau assumes that only social man wages war against himself, and that there is nothing natural in this. Rousseau also argues that humanity in their natural condition would not be predisposed to war because people have a natural empathy towards each other: 'It is this compassion that hurries us without reflection to the relief of those who are in distress: it is this which, in the state of nature, supplies the place of laws, mores, and virtue, with the advantage that no one is tempted to disobey its gentle voice' (1973: 68). Whether it is the cry of the child or the shriek of pain of the injured, we are animals that, according to Rousseau, cannot ignore the suffering of others.

So Rousseau sees us as isolated individuals – but as individuals more like animals than the human individuals we see ourselves as today: driven by self-preservation ('the only goods he recognizes in the universe are food, a female and sleep') but not driven to competition and conflict: rather, being motivated by compassion for others, but a compassion that does not have a moral or theological derivation but is simply one of our natural faculties. We can sum this up with a famous Rousseauian distinction: we are motivated by *amour de soi* (love of self, which can include compassion) but not by *amour propre* (selfishness, greed, vanity); the latter is an invention of civilized life, a feature of human existence under certain conditions. Indeed, he says: '[I]t is reason that engenders *amour proper* . . . It is philosophy that isolates him' (1973: 68). But what has caused the conditions that have turned our natural compassion into selfishness?

One of the most radical and profound claims in Rousseau is that private property, once established within the state of nature, has led to inequality and the creation of social and political institutions that further deepen inequality and stunt human development. 'The first man who, having enclosed a piece of ground, bethought to himself of saying, "This is mine", and found people simple enough to believe him, was the real founder of civil society' (1973: 76). Now, so long as property acquisition and maintenance can be carried out solely by individuals, people in the state of nature can continue to live 'free, healthy, honest and happy lives . . . But from the moment one man began to stand in need of the help of another . . . slavery and misery were soon seen to germinate with the crops' (1973: 83).

Rousseau therefore provides an account of how various 'material' drives to move beyond the state of nature have inaugurated a new psychology in humanity. Individuals are no longer simply creatures that love themselves; they have begun to recognize that if humanity can elevate itself above other animals, then there must also be distinctions within humanity: 'by looking upon his species as of the highest order, he prepared the way for assuming pre-eminence as an individual' (1973: 78). Humanity's natural *amour de soi* has begun to change into *amour propre*: natural self-love and compassion are replaced by social vanity and competition.

Rousseau continues the story. Metallurgy and agriculture have brought the great revolution that decisively took humanity out of the natural condition: '[I]t was iron and corn which first civilized men and which ruined humanity' (1973: 83). Those who owned the means to produce iron and corn became the first great property owners, the first class of men to enslave other men. But Rousseau argues that this slavery must have been precarious, so the next great social revolution enshrined the rights of the property owners in the apparatus of government. Government therefore emerged as a kind of confidence trick instituted by the wealthy and powerful to protect their resources from those without property by claiming that government would benefit all. The poor 'all ran headlong to their chains, in hopes of securing their liberty' (1973: 89).

Possessions, scarcity, natural disasters and human psychology have led humanity from a natural condition of savagery into the world of civilization, according to Rousseau. Hobbes considered broadly similar qualities, such as scarcity and vanity, to be those which provided the motivation for conflict and the route out of the state of nature (thanks to reason) and towards life under government; Rousseau understood these features to be at the very core of our *civilization*, including our contemporary political institutions. According to Rousseau, it is wrong even to imply that humanity may have agreed to its current social and political arrangements by way of a social contract. Instead, society has developed forms of political organization that reflect basic inequalities as mankind emerged from their original condition of savagery. There has not yet been a social contract where all can will a life without the perils of inequality, according to Rousseau. There has not yet been a contract that will take us beyond the inequalities of so-called civilized life:

The inequality which now prevails owes its strength and growth to the development of our faculties and the advance of the human mind, and becomes at last permanent and legitimate by the establishment of property and the laws. (1973: 105)

We are building a picture of Rousseau as a critic of the *political* nature of the liberal depictions of our (allegedly) 'natural condition'. At the heart of this is an account of the development of private property, and an analysis of its effects, that makes the liberal goal of instituting political life to secure private property a means of instituting the inequality that private property embodies. There is no doubt that private property has been the motor for the development of 'civilized society', but 'how civilized are we?' asks Rousseau. Humanity is stunted, believing itself to be free when it is enslaved; believing that government serves the people when it serves only those with property; believing that reason leads to emancipation when in fact the reason that drives selfishness and individualism leads only to further misery for the mass of society; believing that increasing specialization leads to technological advance when in fact it divides society against itself. As humanity has emerged from its natural condition to become 'civilized', now it must go beyond the inequalities of civilization and reach for the true freedom that emerges from being untied – in a polity that speaks with one voice for all, not just for some. For Rousseau, what is needed is:

> . . . a form of association which will defend and protect with the whole common force the person and the goods of each associate and in which each, whilst uniting himself with all, may still obey himself alone and be as free as before . . . The clauses, properly understood, may be reduced to one – the total alienation of each associate, together with all his rights, to the whole community . . . the alienation being without reserve, the union is as perfect as it can be. (1973: 174)

In one sense this has a Hobbesian ring to it – the alienation of rights granted to a sovereign body – and in another sense we can see an almost Lockean construction of the contract, the alienation of rights to the community. But these similarities should not blind us to the 'clear water' between the earlier contract theorists and Rousseau. In Hobbes, the contract binds each individual with every other to create a sovereign authority that *rules over* all individuals. In Locke, the contract binds each individual with every other to create an arbiter to *rule over* them, in the (possibly broad) domain of property rights; yes, government can overstep the bounds of the contract by going beyond the protection of private property, and in such cases sovereign authority reverts to the community, but only so that a newly legitimate government can be formed to *rule over* the people. Rousseau's version is different because he argues that the social contract that is needed to vitiate the inequalities of social life must be one that establishes a political community that *rules over itself*.

How does this theory resolve the problems of inequality, selfishness and human dependency that have grown as civilization has 'advanced'? Initially, Rousseau distinguishes natural liberty, the liberty in the state of nature (which has come to be confused with dependency) from moral liberty, the real liberty found in being one's own master (1973: 178). Natural liberty is about following our instincts and desires, our appetites and impulses; being master of oneself is about being the author of laws that we can follow rationally. As Rousseau says: '[T]he mere impulse of appetite is slavery, whilst obedience to a law which we prescribe to ourselves is liberty' (1973: 178). But how does this idea of freedom become embodied in collective political life? 'Each of us,' he says, 'puts his person and all his power in common under the supreme direction of the general will, and in our corporate capacity, we receive each member as an indivisible part of the whole' (1973: 175).

One of the most important consequences of the social contract is that humanity undergoes a transformation in its nature as we come to express the general will of the community. What is the general will? The contrast is with the idea of private will, and especially with the idea that the sum of private wills can guide society. (Adam Smith's 'hidden hand' argument in defence of the free-market is effectively that the sum of private acts will lead to the greater good for all of society.) Rather, the general will is the articulation of the common good. Ian Hampsher-Monk well expresses the demanding nature of this concept when he defines the general will in Rousseau as follows: '[T]he general will is what the sovereign assembly of all citizens ought to decide, if its deliberations were as they should be' (1992: 180). Rousseau puts it like this: '[T]he sovereign, merely by virtue of what it is, is always what it should be' (1973: 177). The general will, in other words, is the expression of the common good by virtue of three particular features. First, it sustains society (the general will is the bond of the community, the source of what is required to construct a real community); secondly, it brings about equality (the general will cannot, by definition, be the imposition of the will of some against others); and thirdly, it applies to all (the community as a whole is subject to the general will because the community itself exerts that will, and no individual can remove himself from it).

Problematically, though, Rousseau argues that 'whoever refuses to obey the general will shall be compelled to do so by the whole body. This means nothing less than that he will be forced to be free' (1973: 177). Does this mean that the very idea of the general will sanctions deeply illiberal, possibly totalitarian, outcomes? Before rushing to condemn Rousseau for this conclusion, clarity is required. The key issue is not that Rousseau's state can and should coerce citizens, because all states do this. What we might object to in Rousseau's formulation is the claim that in coercing subjects, the state might be forcing them to be *free*. Consider the analogy of addiction, however. If we use drastic measures to coerce someone to end their habit of smoking, then are we forcing them to be free on the grounds that we have prevented a life of addiction and dependency? Abstractly, at least, coercion and freedom may not be contradictory. But is the same true in the world of politics? Extending the analogy of addiction, we could argue that if a democracy were about to abrogate its sovereign authority to a tyrant then violent intervention to prevent this may be a case of 'forcing' a whole people to be free. Underlying such examples is Rousseau's 'positive' account of freedom as self-mastery. Is it not correct to say that as one becomes more rational, and moves from childishness to maturity, then one becomes free from childish irrationalities? Is this not true at a collective level as well? In a society that has emerged from civil strife and barbarity, one that has been stunted by the reign of private property since its inception, one would expect that some individuals will have trouble orienting their thinking to 'the general will'. It seems plausible, therefore, that such individuals will have difficulty realizing their true moral and civil freedoms as equal members of a harmonious polity. Perhaps, therefore, it is not only legitimate but necessary to force some individuals to be free by helping them to think with the viewpoint of all, rather than from their own particular and selfish perspective.

We have touched on Rousseau's vision, and considered his critique of inequality within society, his dislike of the dependency that results from inequality, and his arguments for a new form of society based on equality where the freedom of individuals is expressed in following laws of their own making, so that individuals are, finally, truly independent. This idea of freedom as independence is the core of

Rousseau's political philosophy, intertwined with a critique of private property, the idea of the general will as the expression of the common good, and a view of human nature that centres on what we are capable of becoming, rather than simply what we are. All these ideas contribute to a reading of Rousseau as a radical critic of social-contract liberalism from within the tradition itself. Rousseau's political philosophy also paves the way for more radical critiques of the state, which were to break free of the confines of the social contract tradition in order to really describe the power of the state. It is to such ideas that we turn in the next chapter.

CHAPTER 3

THE STATE AND POWER

Getting the balance right between authority and liberty is difficult, not least because we invest our power in an authority which then tends to use it for its own ends. In modern times, we call this the state. While we may try to hold it in check, experience would suggest that the state has a tendency towards securing its own autonomy, not necessarily those of the people who have (allegedly) authorized it. Increasingly differentiated from society, the state wields power as if it were a mighty person bearing down upon us. Hobbes captured this sense of state power in his characterization of the monstrous 'leviathan' created by individuals but then set loose to do as it pleases. There's no doubt that many people to this day feel that 'the state' is not there to protect their liberty, but rather it is an overbearing power bent on curtailing their liberty at every turn. However, the nature of the state and the power it possesses are not easily characterized; in fact, these are deeply contentious issues in political philosophy. The focus in this chapter will be on theoretical frameworks that provide critical accounts of the relationship between the state and power: Marxism, feminism and poststructuralism. Before getting into these discussions, however, it is worth saying a few words about the idea of the state itself.

The state is a distinctly modern form of political organization (although some political philosophers and political scientists prefer to use state as the word for all forms of political organization, in which case they will talk about 'the modern state'). In Europe, states began to emerge from amongst the diffuse centres of power that characterized medieval Christendom. These states were established as bounded territories to be treated as sovereign entities; that is, entities that had supreme power over their own affairs. Michael Oakeshott, however, gives a more expansive definition of the state. The defining features of the state, according to Oakeshott (1991), are that it is authorized to rule over people, that it has the power to do so vested in 'the apparatus of governing', and that the people who are ruled are obligated to each other as citizens – that is, we are obligated as members of a political community rather than, for example, as followers of the same religion, or members of the same tribe or family. We should add that one of the defining features of a state is that it uses its authority and power within a territory as a basis upon which to found external, or what we usually call international, relations with other states. Indeed, the Treaties of Westphalia in 1648 that ended the Thirty Years' War are usually thought to be the defining historical moment when a Europe of states was first acknowledged as having been established.

What these remarks reveal is that the state is two-sided: it embodies power *over* the people within its territory, and it expresses the power *of* the people as it acts 'on their behalf'. While not contradictory, as we saw in the last chapter, this dual aspect is worthy of further investigation. Indeed, for many political philosophers the nexus of power that the state embodies within it, is expressive of deeper undercurrents of power at work within our social, economic and even gender relations. In order to understand the state, we need to grasp the way power operates within and through the state. One of the most compelling accounts of where the 'real' power of the state resides is found in the work of Karl Marx.

THE CAPITALIST STATE

Turning our attention to Marx, we will see that the historical dimension of political theory that Rousseau began to develop (see Chapter 2) becomes much more explicit, and more complicated, but also (I suggest) more rewarding and challenging. In particular, what we will refer to as Marx's 'materialist conception of history' casts new light on the role of the state in modern political life by conceiving of it as 'a committee for managing the common affairs of the whole bourgeoisie' (McLellan, 2000: 247). In order to show that such bold claims are not mere rhetorical flourishes, though they are that as well, it is necessary to reconstruct Marx's political philosophy with some care; all the while, though, maintaining a focus on his remarks about the power of the state.

We can begin with a brief history of philosophy. Eighteenth-century German philosopher Immanuel Kant is a pivotal figure in the development of modern philosophy because his critique of rationalism and empiricism (revealing the shared assumptions that motivate these apparently different philosophical positions) inaugurated a new critical method in philosophy which had as its primary task the delineation of what we can legitimately know, as human beings about the world – and, conversely, what as humans we can never know about the world. For Georg W. F. Hegel, writing at the dawn of the nineteenth century, Kant's critical philosophy was inspirational but ultimately too meek. According to Hegel, philosophers must never rest content with setting up limits to knowledge, or with demarcating whole areas of inquiry as simply unknowable. Philosophy, for Hegel, is a search for absolute knowledge or it is nothing. However, the search for absolute knowledge is not one that philosophers could conduct, as it were, from a distance. For Hegel, philosophy is a form of thought and thought is part of the world, so knowing the world and knowing philosophy become part of the same process (otherwise there would be a limit, a demarcation or division between 'philosophy' and 'thought' and 'the world' that would prevent absolute knowledge). Importantly, Hegel conceived of the search for absolute knowledge as a *process*: the history of the world unfolds and as it does so philosophy unfolds alongside it, each 'overlapping' the other in complex ways. What is the underlying force that keeps history and ideas moving? Hegel calls it the 'power of the negative', and this power means that historical development and the development of ideas are spurred on by opposition and tension. Every time some new phenomenon, way of life or idea comes into existence, the possibility of its negation, its opposite, emerges as well. For example, as the revolutionary ideals of the French Republic were declared in 1789, Edmund Burke was already marshalling the treatise that gave birth to modern conservatism: his *Reflections on the Revolution in France*. The tension between the emergence of the new and the emergence of its opposite gives momentum to history because the tension that emerges between, say, revolutionary republicanism and conservatism is one that people strive to overcome in the hope of synthesizing the best of these opposing ideas. Of course, any new synthesis of opposing forces that emerges will bring a new opposition to the fore and humanity, according to Hegel, is again impelled to resolve this new tension, and so on until an ultimate synthesis is achieved which means there are no oppositions or tensions left. At this point, according to Hegel, humanity will have achieved its full realization – a life without tension, contradiction or limits – and we will finally have absolute knowledge of the world and our place in it. The patterned movement of history and thought progressing towards a final resolution of all opposition is what Hegel calls *dialectics*.

Hegel's *Phenomenology of Spirit* is an account of how, if you begin with the simplest idea that things are given in the here and now and given immediately to our senses, this necessarily gives rise to a series of oppositions and tensions that lead human reason towards the idea of absolute knowledge (an account that weaves itself in and out of human history in complex ways). However, for all Hegel's bravado and inventiveness, we must note his philosophical lineage. In claiming that we can unravel the history of knowing and the history of the world alongside each other, Hegel was firmly positioning his ideas within the tradition of what philosophers now call German idealism. Idealism is the claim that we know the world by knowing the ideas we have of the world. Kant's subject-centred approach to knowledge had inaugurated this tradition and, as we have seen, the difficulty that accompanies this idealism is that it means that we cannot know anything of the world as it really is: we know how it appears to us, but not how it is in itself. Hegel's dialectical approach represents the culmination of this tradition, because it claims that we can overcome this barrier within the idealist tradition if we chart the development of mind and thought through history towards its ultimate reconciliation with the world as it is. Kant, in other words, had misunderstood the historically contingent limits of our knowledge, seeing them as universal limits; Hegel argued that the development of human understanding was necessarily bound to overcome these limits as our ability to reason developed. In *The Philosophy of Right*, his major political treatise, Hegel employed his dialectical method to discuss social and political life. The culmination of social and political existence, Hegel argued, is the modern state: it is the perfectly rational form for harmonizing the competing claims of individual freedom and collective freedom. Hegel is a defender of positive freedom: 'I am truly free when the other is also free and is recognized by me as free' (1971: 171). The mechanism for this mutual recognition is the collective life we are capable of living within a state. To the extent that law embodies this recognition, the state itself is truly free and rational, and all people are able to fulfil their own potential as free beings, acting together within it. In a rationally organized free state:

> . . . man is recognised and treated as a rational being, as free, as a person; and the individual, on his side, makes himself worthy of this recognition by overcoming the natural state of his self-consciousness and obeying a universal, the will that in essence and actuality will, the law; he behaves, therefore, towards others in a manner that is universally valid, recognizing them – as he wishes others to recognize him – as free, as persons. (1971: 172)

A sovereign authority has authority, therefore, precisely to the extent that it expresses the universal desire to be recognized and to recognize others as free and rational beings. Any state that does not treat everybody within its territories as free persons is a mutilated or deformed state that will, inevitably, come to dissolve and eventually transform into one in which the freedom of all is enshrined in every fibre of government. We can see the link to Rousseau's conception of the general will, but there is still a significant distance between Rousseau's patchwork historical narrative and Hegel's dialectical logic of historical development. According to Hegel, state authority, fully realized, embodies absolute knowledge to the extent that it is the rational made real and the real made rational. As curious as it may seem to us now, Hegel believed that the absolute form of the state (the rational state made real, the real state made rational) was a constitutional monarchy with a bicameral legislature (a two-tiered law-making body) and a civil service, held together by a system of checks and balances. It fell to Marx to reveal the internal tensions and contradictions in this form of government; and with these divisions and oppositions such a state, by Hegel's own logic, could not be the most rational form of government. Nonetheless, for all that Marx was profoundly critical of Hegel, it is crucial to understand that he adopted Hegel's idea of the dialectical development of history. As we shall see, Marx took the structure Hegel's concept of dialectical logic and historical development but changed the content (Cohen, 1978). We can understand Marx's complex philosophical relationship with Hegel by considering the influence of the lesser-known but important thinker, Ludwig Feuerbach, on Marx's interpretation of Hegel's dialectical method.

In his book *The Essence of Christianity*, Feuerbach invoked what he called 'transformational criticism' in the service of inverting the usual view of the relation between God and humanity. Rather than the theological view that humans are beings created by God, Feuerbach argued that God is an idea conceived by humans. Human beings, according to Feuerbach, create God so as to explain the unexplainable; that is, to posit a world of harmony beyond the chaos and unpredictability of everyday life: 'in religion, man objectifies his own latent nature' (1957: 18). While interesting in itself (and a landmark text in the development of atheism), the important point in relation to the development of Marx's ideas is Feuerbach's argument that the dialectical philosophy of Hegel was, in fact, a form of religion. In a nutshell, Feuerbach argues that idealism is indistinguishable from theological speculation, and as such it too can be unravelled as a form of human endeavour in need of anthropological explanation. Hegel's search for absolute knowledge and his speculative tracking of the mind's progress through history and philosophy, according to Feuerbach, is a form of humanity's self-alienation. The only way to explain why humans would seek such other-worldly certainties is to analyse the material existence of humanity that leads people to place their hopes and dreams in God and/or idealist philosophies of mind. While the more traditional, conservative strain of the immediate response to Hegel consisted of philosophers working through the theological consequences of his work with a view to showing that he had finally and decisively brought religion and science into harmony, Feuerbach took a radically different tack. He proposed a new approach intended to show that Hegel's idealism is not the culmination of philosophy, but merely the end of German idealism in philosophy. Once Hegelian theory is exposed as speculative theology, the way is cleared for a new, human-centred, materialist philosophy to emerge.

There is no doubt that Marx was immediately and profoundly influenced by Feuerbach's anthropological-materialist critique of Hegelian idealism. However, even in the early years when Marx had thoroughly adopted the language and method of Feuerbach – the years when he thought of himself as a Feuerbachian – Marx always had a more socio-political, critical focus. Marx's paragraph-by-paragraph study of Hegel's *Philosophy of Right* is the obvious early example of this, as it shows Marx employing a transformative approach (McLellan, 2000: 33–42). For instance, he reworks Hegel's claim that the state 'determines' civil society by turning it around so that, Marx argues, the state is actually determined by forces within civil society. In Feuerbachian language, Marx argues that Hegel mystified the state 'as a subject' capable of acting as if it were a real person, instead of analysing the state as the consequence of the activities of real people. The tenor of this critique is repeated in a number of the important early texts written by Marx. With regard to his analysis of the state, two of these early texts are worthy of particular mention: 'On the Jewish question' (McLellan, 2000: 46–70) and 'Towards a critique of Hegel's *Philosophy of Right*: Introduction' (McLellan, 2000: 71–82).

The 'Jewish question' that is the subject of the first of these texts emerged as a result of calls for religious freedom for the Jews in mid-nineteenth-century Germany. Bruno Bauer, who was a very influential reader of Hegel's work, responded to these calls by arguing that freedom for the Jews was empty and meaningless unless it was in the context of freedom for everyone in a totally free (German) state. Marx's essay is a response to Bauer which seeks to further radicalize Bauer's apparently radical position. Marx argues that the idea of a state free of religion will not mean the end of religion; therefore, it will not be the end of humanity's alienation from itself (note the influence of Feuerbach again). This idea works itself out in the essay in ways that continue to be pertinent to contemporary political life. Whereas Bauer claimed that political freedom for all was the precondition of emancipation for the Jews, Marx argued that political emancipation was not the same as 'real, human emancipation'. He pointed to the fact that the actually existing secular democracies of his time (the USA and France in particular) were still societies riddled with religious fervour. It was clear, according to Marx, that a secular state could not guarantee freedom from religion because liberal democratic and secular states allowed religion to flourish in the private realm. In this sense, Marx argued, the liberal democratic state acts as the surreptitious guardian of religion's alienation of humanity from its own real potential. A free state, therefore, is not simply one that is free from religion in political life, it is one that has managed to overcome religion in society as well.

In 'On the Jewish question', Marx's critique of Hegel is rather oblique, coming as it does through the critique of Bauer. During these early years, however, Marx was engaged in a detailed and prolonged investigation of Hegel's *Philosophy of Right*. The 'Introduction', written some months after the detailed reading mentioned above, provides a key source for his relationship with Hegel. In this text, Marx argues (as, at the time, a good Feuerbachian) that criticism of religion is the prerequisite of all social and political criticism. It is not just that religious authorities had such a strong hold on political authorities, though they did in Marx's Germany; it is rather that, in the wake of Hegel, the critique of religion must be a philosophical prerequisite of all critique because of the religious dimension of Hegel's appeal to absolute knowledge. That said, Marx does turn his attention to the details of Hegel's rational state to argue that Hegel's defence of the bureaucrats as the neutral and therefore universal class of social and political life (the class able to express the interests of all) was lamentably lacking in a grasp of the realities of bureaucratic administrations, because they tended to serve their own interests rather than those of the people. Nonetheless, Marx does adopt the notion of a universal class, and it is in this text that we witness the first stirrings of an idea that will forever bear his name: the proletariat, he argues, are the class of people that carry the interests of all in their labouring power and relationships. As such, and joining up the themes of 'On the Jewish question', Marx argues that real, human emancipation will only come about as the proletariat gain control of the state – control that must be won through revolutionary upheaval.

Before continuing to outline the development of these ideas in Marx, it is worth just pausing again to reflect on his relationship with Hegel and Feuerbach. Having used Feuerbach's ideas to aid his criticism of Hegel's idealism, Marx became increasingly dissatisfied with Feuerbach's materialism itself. While he could not agree with Hegel's idealism, he did feel the force of Hegel's dialecticism. This is an extract from Marx's 'Theses on Feuerbach':

> The chief defect of all hitherto existing materialism (that of Feuerbach included) is that the thing, reality, sensuousness, is conceived only in the form of the object or of contemplation, but not as sensuous human activity, practice, not subjectively. Hence, in contradistinction to materialism, the active side was developed abstractly by idealism – which, of course, does not know real sensuous activity as such. (McLellan, 2000: 171)

In fact, Marx felt that he had synthesized the best elements of two opposing traditions – dialectical idealism and anthropological materialism – and the result is often called dialectical materialism (though Marx rarely used the term himself). A dialectical and materialist understanding of history is a 'grand narrative' (see Chapter 7) of the historical development of human relations on the 'real' basis of human productivity, rather than the illusory basis of Hegel's conception of 'mind' or 'spirit', using a logic of opposition heading towards an end-point (rather than Feuerbach's static anthropological generalizations). However, it may well be that Marx's synthesis of these two traditions was not so much his great achievement as his conceptual undoing. This was the conclusion of many philosophers in the twentieth century who argued that the source of Hegel's idealism was not only or evenly chiefly in his latent religiosity, it was in the dialectical method itself. It may be that there is something intrinsically idealist about dialectical logic, such that 'dialectical materialism' is actually a contradiction in terms. Nonetheless, the development of Marx's early ideas can be understood in terms of his Feuerbachian critique of Hegel (from idealism to materialism) and his Hegelian critique of Feuerbach (from static materialism to dynamic or dialectical materialism). But having established that Marx broadly shares Hegel's historical outlook, it is worth considering how Marx articulated the materialist content within the dialectical structure. What, in other words, did Marx consider to be the 'real' driving force of history?

In Hegel's philosophical system, the logical driving force of history was the power of the negative as manifested in actual struggles for recognition; that is, in people striving to be recognized as fully-fledged individuals in a world where everyone is similarly identified. Marx argues that this is typical of Hegel's overly idealist analysis of human interaction; Hegel fails to acknowledge that humans' need to labour in the world, and to do so with each other, in order to survive, is even more basic than the desire for recognition. If we do not produce the means of our subsistence then we could not possibly express the desire to be recognized. Therefore, Marx argues, the real motor of history, the form of human interaction that really propels history forward, is a struggle over productive labour. This manifests itself as a struggle between economic classes: 'The history of all hitherto existing society is the history of class struggle' (McLellan, 2000: 246). In simple terms, there has always been conflict within society between those who controlled what was produced and those who produced it. Interestingly, the further back one goes the more complicated the picture is, in terms of multiple and overlapping gradations or classes of people. However, the emergence of capitalism from feudalism brought with it a simplification of class antagonism that, according to Marx, had gradually divided the whole of humanity into 'two hostile camps': bourgeois and proletarian. The bourgeois are the minority who own the means of production, and the proletariat are the vast majority who have to sell their labour to the bourgeoisie in order to survive. According to Marx, this is the underlying opposition in contemporary society that no amount of tinkering with the democratic credentials of the liberal state will resolve on its own. As long as people have to sell a part of themselves, their labour, to others, there can never be real 'recognition amongst equals'. Consequently, the solution to class antagonism is not to be found within the modern democratic state but in a post-capitalist economic system: 'In place of the old bourgeois society, with its classes and class antagonisms, we shall have an association, in which the free development of each is the condition for the free development of all' (McLellan, 2000: 262). In a post-capitalist economic order there will be no classes and without classes, without antagonism, there will be no need for a state to broker the competing interests of individuals and classes. In due course, the state will simply 'wither away' (McLellan, 2000: 223).

While such utopian claims are integral to Marx's political philosophy (because they represent his direct inheritance of Hegelian dialectics), it is true to say that Marx wisely did not dwell too much on what post-capitalist life might be like. He did, however, reflect extensively on the role of the state in capitalist societies. In general, Marx argues that 'all struggles within the state, the struggle between democracy, aristocracy and monarchy, the struggle for the franchise etc. are merely illusory forms in which the real struggles of the different classes are fought out amongst each other' (McLellan, 2000: 169). More pointedly, these are illusory forms that serve the underlying aims of the bourgeoisie by both distracting from the real struggles and by naturalizing the competition between people that capitalism requires in order to sustain itself. The state, in other words, has an ideological purpose and the various attempts to justify state authority (such as the social contract theories of the previous chapter) are really ideological props supporting the interests of capital: 'What else does the history of ideas prove, than that intellectual production changes its character in proportion as material production is changed? The ruling ideas of each age have ever been the ideas of its ruling class' (McLellan, 2000: 260).

Liberal attempts to justify state power are premised upon the assumptions such as that competition is natural, that inequality based on property ownership is natural, that the free market itself is a natural phenomenon, and that greed can be good: according to Marx, such assumptions simply serve the purpose of legitimating not the state but the accumulation of massive wealth by a small minority who own the means of production, and the great immiseration of the vast majority who do not. The following passage from *The German Ideology* sums up Marx's view of the state well:

> If power is taken as the basis of right, as Hobbes etc. do, then right, law etc. are merely the symptom, the expression of other relations upon which State power rests. The material life of individuals, which by no means depends merely on their 'will', [rather] their mode of production and form of intercourse, which mutually determine each other – this is the real basis of the State and remains so at all stages at which division of labour and private property are still necessary, quite independently of the will of individuals. These actual relations are in no way created by the State power; on the contrary, they are the power creating it. (McLellan, 2000: 184)

THE PATRIARCHAL STATE

What if Marx has misunderstood the real nature of state power? Perhaps the state is not primarily a political expression of an economic division in society, but an organization that maintains an even deeper division between people: the division between men and women, and the subordination of the latter by the former? After all, there is a telling lack of concern for women in Marx's work (though his collaborator and co-author Frederick Engels was rather more aware of the need to address the situation of women). According to Catharine MacKinnon:

> Marx ridiculed treating value and class as if they were natural givens. He bitingly criticized theories that treated class as if it arose spontaneously and operated mechanistically yet harmoniously in accord with natural laws. He identified such theories as justifications for an unjust status quo. Yet this is exactly the way he treated gender. Even when women produced commodities as

waged labour, Marx wrote about them primarily as mothers, housekeepers, and members of the weaker sex. His work shares with liberal theory the view that women naturally belong where they are socially placed. (1989: 13)

Without going into the details of her critique of Marx, this section will follow MacKinnon through her critique of the liberal state as a defender of patriarchal power. A practising lawyer, academic and activist, MacKinnon has done work on the state which has been very influential in questioning the liberal ideals of abstract equality and rights. As we will see, one of the examples she uses to problematize these ideals is the 'paradoxical' legislation surrounding pornography.

Liberal theory and liberal democratic states place a high value on equality, especially on equal treatment before the law. Quite simply, it is one of the pillars of liberal ideology that the law should treat everyone equally. It is this pillar of liberal ideology that MacKinnon subjects to criticism from a feminist perspective. She highlights what she takes to be a contradiction at the core of liberal sex equality legislation. In her own words:

Socially, one tells a woman from a man by their difference from each other, but a woman is legally recognised to be discriminated against on the basis of sex only when she can first be said to be like a man . . . Sex equality becomes a contradiction in terms, something of an oxymoron. (1989: 216)

In pursuing a claim of unequal treatment because of sexual discrimination a woman has to prove how she has been treated differently because she is a woman, but only by first being asked to consider whether a man 'in the same situation' would have been rewarded or punished in the same way, for example in terms of pay or promotion. According to MacKinnon, this demand actually negates the differences between the sexes which are deemed to have brought about the problem in the first place. She goes on to argue that this contradictory demand implies a confusing understanding of sex/gender within the law. Legal frameworks recognize certain differences between the sexes as natural and fixed, other differences as the product of society and therefore as potentially arbitrary. The sex equality legislation is supposed to remove the latter on the grounds that such arbitrary differentiation amounts to 'sex discrimination'. But to call this 'sex discrimination' is confusing, and this confusion all too often results in women's claims being represented as claims that are not the subject of law because they ultimately revolve around 'natural sexual difference'. In other words, discrimination in terms of socially constructed gender roles is often represented as a case of natural sexual difference which the law cannot act upon or legislate against. In this way, tensions within liberal legal frameworks about the relationship between sex and gender serve to uphold the inherently patriarchal power of the legal system.

But what of the raft of 'affirmative action' policies that have now found their way into liberal legislation? Is it not the case that liberal states have now enshrined legal protection for 'difference', rather than simply legal redress for 'discrimination'? In all sectors of public life and many areas of private business, gender differences are supposed to be actively promoted and celebrated. MacKinnon argues, however, that the legal affirmation of difference does not radically solve the contradiction underpinning the legal equality arguments. In her own words:

> Gender might not even code as difference, might not mean distinction epistemologically, were it not for its consequences for social power. Distinctions of body or mind or behaviour are pointed to as cause rather than effect, with no realization that they are so deeply effect rather than cause that pointing to them at all is an effect. Inequality comes first; difference comes after . . . If this is so, a discourse and a law of gender that centre on difference serve as ideology to neutralize, rationalize, and cover disparities of power, even as they appear to criticize or problematize them. Difference is the velvet glove on the iron fist of domination. (1989: 219)

In short, to idealize gender difference is to support the structures of gender inequality that lead to the idea that the genders are 'different' in the first place. For MacKinnon, both the 'sameness' and the 'difference' strands of liberal legislation conceal the reality that 'man is the measure of all things'. Either 'woman' is measured against man and found to be the same, or 'woman' is measured against man and found to be different. The sameness/difference approaches provide 'two ways for the law to hold women to a male standard and to call that sex equality' (1989: 221).

A defender of the liberal state might well respond to MacKinnon along these lines: in identifying the inadequacies of the liberal system as its stands, MacKinnon shows how formal equalities (based on either sameness or difference) need to be rethought in order to promote real, substantive equality in social and political life. The best way for this to be done is to appeal to the liberal doctrine of human rights; after all, using the discourse of rights has been fundamental in bringing about positive changes in the legal systems of liberal democracies for centuries. MacKinnon, however, claims that the discourse of rights is as problematic as the sex equality legislation.

Echoing Marx, she argues that 'to be a person, an abstract individual with abstract rights, may be a bourgeois concept, but its content is male' (1989: 229). In a manner similar to her arguments about sex equality, MacKinnon asserts that a 'woman's right' is either a right to be like a man, or a right to be different from a man; either way, the concept of 'man' remains the measure, and therefore gives content to the formal idea of rights. Bringing these issues together, 'abstract equality has never included those rights that women as women most need and never have had' (1989: 229). Moreover, liberal rights are assigned to individuals as individuals. Consequently, these rights do not recognize that the harm inflicted on individuals, harm that rights are supposed to protect against, often has a structural rather than an individual basis. For example, the harm inflicted on women in liberal democratic (and other) states has its basis not only in patriarchally-minded individuals, but also in the system of patriarchy itself. So to claim a right in a liberal context is to accept that the harm is defined as an 'individuated, atomistic, linear, exclusive, isolated, narrowly tort like – in a word, positivistic' way (1989: 208). But the harm committed against women, argues MacKinnon, is not always of this sort because it finds its sources, justifications and expressions in the patriarchal structures of everyday life. This indicates a further problem with the defence of liberal rights. Liberal rights are typically conceived negatively: that is, individuals have rights against the over-reaching arms of the state. This assumes that everyday life is basically well-ordered and that it is only when the state breaches that order that we can legitimately invoke our rights against it. This, for MacKinnon, patently overlooks the fact that the society is patriarchal to its core. In contrast to the mainstream liberal view of rights, MacKinnon offers an alternative (liberal?) view of rights as a means to the end of achieving real substantive equality, not just formal equality before the law. 'Women's rights' understood in this way would not be rights against the state, or against individuals (men or women), but rights to secure an end to patriarchal social structures. A right would be a right for equality, MacKinnon says, not against inequality.

We can see some of these issues at work in MacKinnon's analysis and critique of pornography. This is how she defines pornography:

> In contemporary industrial society, pornography is an industry that mass produces sexual intrusion on, access to, possession and use of women by men for men for profit. It exploits women's sexual and economic inequality for gain. It sells women to men as and for sex. It is a technologically sophisticated traffic in women. (1989: 195)

This definition immediately takes us away from the idea that pornography is solely a form of representation. The usual discourses about pornography tend to assume that it is a form of representation, and then argue about whether particular representations are erotic or pornographic. In law, this view of pornography is embodied in the idea of obscenity. MacKinnon argues, however, that 'the obscenity standard is built on what the male standpoint sees'. This is not only because most judges are men, though that is true; it has more to do with the fact that the pornographic image of a woman (primarily, the common pornographic image of a woman enjoying forced sex) is so deeply embedded in the social structures of contemporary life that the very idea of trying to differentiate eroticism from pornography in terms of obscenity seems pointless. '[P]ornography,' she says, 'institutionalizes the sexuality of male supremacy, which fuses the eroticization of dominance and submission with the social construction of male and female' (1989: 197). Therefore 'men's obscenity is not woman's pornography. Obscenity is more concerned with whether men blush, pornography with whether women bleed' (1989: 199). Given this, MacKinnon argues, pornography is not based on an idea of the right or wrong way to represent sex, but is actually a central part of a process of structured inequality that harms women in general. As such, 'the issue is not what the harm of pornography is, but how the harm of pornography is to become visible' because 'to the extent that pornography succeeds in constructing social reality, it becomes invisible as harm' (1989: 204).

What of free speech, the archetypal liberal freedom? Although aspects of the pornography industry may harm some women, is it possible to rectify these infringements and abuses while also retaining the central liberal goal of providing a legal environment that secures free speech? Given MacKinnon's account of pornography as an integral feature of the patriarchal structuring of social reality, the liberal appeal to free speech, either in defence of pornography or in debates about whether to limit pornography as a violation of free speech, is rendered meaningless because the 'free-speech of men silences the free-speech of women' (1989: 205). At stake, according to MacKinnon, is the underlying claim that pornography is a way of securing a male sexualized image of woman as part of the social reality of being a woman. To argue from a liberal perspective that representations of sex are pornographic only when they are obscene, or that pornography is permissible as long as there is no direct harm to an individual, or that it can only be criminalized as an instance of some other crime (for example, an act of violence) – all these arguments overlook the fact that 'pornography does not work sexually without gender hierarchy'. The repeated refrain of MacKinnon's critique of the liberal democratic legal frameworks of the modern state is that they ignore the fundamental (that is, structural and systematic) inequality between the sexes that orders society hierarchically. Liberal responses to sex inequalities wrongly assume a level playing field to start with; MacKinnon argues that a patriarchal playing field was established long ago and that the modern state sustains that inequality, thereby opposing women's claims for real equality. We will see later (Chapter 7) that many feminists would see the patriarchal playing field as being grounded not 'just' in structural inequalities deeply embedded within society, but actually in the very fabric of the 'symbolic order' that makes society possible at all.

THREE DIMENSIONS OF POWER

Though Marx and MacKinnon provide compelling reasons for believing that the state serves the interests of a particular class and/ or gender rather than being simply a body authorized to protect our liberties, there is a sense that these broad critiques of the modern liberal state do not really give a sufficiently nuanced account of power. Maybe we need this more nuanced account if we are to understand how the state functions. It was with the birth of political science (in the wake of the behavioural revolution in the social sciences in the 1950s) that theorists of a more positivist bent attempted to get beyond what they saw as vague definitions of such concepts as class and power, and towards a definition of power that could be measured and quantified. In particular, attention was focused on the American liberal democratic state of the 1950s and 1960s.

It was Robert Dahl's groundbreaking work *Who Governs? Democracy and Power in an American City* (1961) that set off a debate which would become known as the faces or dimensions of power debate. Dahl, an American political scientist, was researching the distribution of power in post-World War Two American political life. In particular, he was trying to find out if power was 'in the hands of' a central governmental elite or dispersed across a plurality of smaller elite groups. In order to pursue this research from the perspective of a political scientist, he proposed a definition of power that could be 'operationalized' in empirical research. He called it 'the intuitive idea of power': 'A has power over B to the extent that A can get B to do something that B would not otherwise do', where A and B are symbols for the political actors involved in various sectors of government. These may be individual people or 'individual groups of people'; we might say today, for example, that Gordon Brown's 'kitchen cabinet' (the small group of advisors and ministers that he trusts most) have power over the cabinet as a whole. Dahl's conclusion was that power was not concentrated in the hands of one elite, but rather dispersed across a plurality of elite groups – hence the label 'pluralist', as opposed to 'elitist', for his analysis of American politics.

Clearly, the strength of Dahl's definition is that it is a neat formulation of our common-sense view of power: a person or group has it, and uses it to get other people or groups to do things they would not otherwise do. This understanding seems intuitively correct and politically relevant, and it has the added bonus of giving political scientists a framework within which to construct research programmes that measure the flow of power in contemporary political institutions. But power is not easily defined. Even within the subsequent pluralist/elitist literature, there emerged an important addition to Dahl's intuitive view: one that supported a 'neo-elitist' view of American democracy. This view is associated with (amongst others) Bacharach and Baratz (1962), a pair of political scientists who argued that Dahl's view of power, and how it operates, overlooked crucial ways in which elites are able to manipulate the political environment around them in order to get what they want. For these two theorists Dahl's definition of power needed extending to take account of such manipulation, and they proposed the following: 'A has power over B to the extent that A can get B to do something that B would not otherwise do *and* A has power over B to the extent that A can limit the scope of decision making by manipulating dominant community values'. They referred to their addition as 'the second face of power'. The most obvious example of this additional dimension of power is 'agenda-setting'. Imagine a situation where A (the government) exercises power over B (the unions) by virtue of 'setting the agenda' for their meetings together. In this way, the government ensures that certain topics and issues which the unions want to discuss are kept off the agenda so that the government can, for example, ease the passage of a piece of legislation to which the unions are opposed. Of course, this kind of agenda-setting is rarely explicit as it is usually done in the 'corridors of power': the smoke-filled rooms and bars of the House of Commons or the US Congress, for example. This second face or dimension of power, therefore, brings to light the way power operates through informal political alliances and 'behind the scenes' deals which shape the formal discussions and debates. Indeed, 'agenda-setting' also occurs in a broader sense: framing the issues that we care about, that we think are worthy of discussion, that reflect our 'values', and so on. Put like this, we can see that power can be wielded by 'the state' as skilful elites manipulate public opinion in pursuit of their own ends. The contemporary phenomenon of the 'spin-doctor' is the most obvious manifestation of this face of power.

Both the first and second dimensions described above assume that power is exercised by political actors against other political actors who are treated as individuals – that is, treated as if they were acting like individuals. But if power operates in the agenda-setting way, it makes sense to extend how we think about power beyond this individualist assumption. For example, if A and B agree on the agenda (taking it quite literally for the moment), does it mean that there is no power at work, that the agenda has not been 'set'? Could it not be that the 'manipulation' is not only 'manipulation of the agenda' but also of the more fundamental 'agreement' on which any political agenda must be based? It may be, for instance, that the 'dominant community values' of Bacharach and Baratz's definition might *already* be an expression of the power of A over B such that the dominant values really do 'dominate'.

This argument was developed by Steven Lukes in his book *Power: A Radical View* (1974). Accepting that power does operate as Dahl, Bacharach and Baratz suggest it does, Lukes nonetheless argues that there is more to the operation of power in society than either or both of the first and second dimensions are able to capture. In particular, he draws on the ideas of Italian Marxist Antonio Gramsci to argue that power is often exercised through 'hegemonic strategies'. These are political-economic strategies that 'manufacture consent' amongst a population. If one accepts, with Gramsci, that the agreement of the people can be manufactured by the state, then it is possible that the people might agree to a course of action (B may 'willingly' agree to do what A wants) and the people and the state may agree on the appropriate remit of the agenda (because A and B recognize their shared community values) but still power may be exercised such that those agreements are 'manufactured' or constructed through dominant organs of power within society such as education, churches and the media – what Louis Althusser, a later French Marxist, referred to as parts of the 'ideological state apparatus'.

Seeking to clarify these Marxist ideas but also preserve their critical normative intent, Lukes defines power as follows: 'A has power over B when A is able to get B to act in a manner contrary to B's real, objective interests'. His aim is to show that the preferences of political actors are always already shaped by their interaction within the public sphere in ways which are not always conscious. He argues that we need to augment the individualist paradigm of power with a broader understanding that power also operates at this deeper, structural level within society. For Lukes, it is clear that our preferences as individuals, and also the preferences of political actors generally, are often shaped by such fundamental structures. These structures, importantly, serve the interests of some and not others: typically, they serve those who benefit from them in terms of increased money, and increased power in the sense of their being able to get what they want. If these structures do not serve the real, objective interests of people then we can say, with Lukes, that power is operating at this structural level.

Of course, there is an important distinction, which Lukes maintains, between what people/political actors may believe, even fervently, is in their best interests, and what is actually in their 'real, objective interests'. A student may think it is in her best interests to work hard at university, so as to get a good job, in order to continue working hard, so that one day she can finally sit in her back garden, having obtained the financial security of a decent pension. However, it may be more in her 'real, objective interests' to work to create an economic and political system in which she does not have to sell her labour to employers, nor engage in dehumanizing and alienating work, in the illusory hope of a blissful retirement. It may indeed be in her real, objective interests to have a full and meaningful working life in which she does not have to sell her labour to others, but can in some other way reap the real rewards of a creative expression of her productive nature. The contentiousness of this example, however, makes it very clear that Lukes' third dimension or face of power has taken us into difficult territory; indeed, the very territory where we started with Marx. Lukes' reliance on 'real, objective interests' implies a normative account of human nature which is heavily indebted to the Marxist tradition, which prioritizes class analysis; are A and B, for Lukes, really economic classes? If so, we have a major problem understanding what is meant by 'real, objective interests'. Perhaps A and B can be treated as genders, and we can return to MacKinnon's analysis? In truth, this political scientific attempt to put the discussion of state power on a sure footing with simple definitions of power has led us back to the Marxist and feminist theories we started with. Is there an alternative way of conceptualizing power, one that might help us to see its relationship with the state in a different light?

POWER AND NORMALIZATION

One route to this alternative conception starts with the assumption that power is not simply used by A against B, or the basis of an artificial agreement between A and B (in A's interests). Rather, it may be that A and B (our various political actors, classes and so on) only exist as political actors because they are the product of networks of power that constitute their identity within the political world. It is the work of Foucault that springs to mind if we follow this line of thought. His view of power takes us away from the traditional models in many respects, and draws our attention to the subtle and often minute ways in which power 'normalizes' our behaviour. It is important to note, however, that Foucault was not responding to the 'dimensions of power' debate. His analysis of power emerged from the distinctive milieu of early-to-mid-1970s France. On the one hand, this was a place still reeling from the massive social upheavals of 'May 1968' (the worker and student uprisings that shook Paris, in particular). More fundamentally, the failure of these uprisings led many on the left of French politics to re-evaluate their critical and intellectual armoury. Could it be that a revolutionary politics of opposition was no longer tenable? Could it be that the social critics had misunderstood the nature of state power? On the other hand, within the academies the dominant structuralist dogma of the time (see Chapter 7) was found wanting, and new approaches were beginning to appear. Foucault's major contribution, in this regard, was to analyse the ways in which power operates across all social relations to shape and condition the structures that give us our sense of identity. Once this subterranean world of power relations was revealed, Foucault argued, we could appreciate both how structures condition our identity (as the structuralists had proposed), and how these structures change over time (which the structuralists tended to deny). In this way, Foucault is a paradigmatic *post*structuralist thinker.

Given this, the challenge which Foucault's ideas posed to traditional models of power can be understood most straightforwardly if we consider his dissatisfaction with both economic and legal approaches to power. He argued that both Marxist and liberal definitions of power tend to oversimplify the operation of power in society, failing to recognize the subtleties which are at work. Of Marxist approaches he says: 'I believe anything can be deduced from the general phenomenon of the domination of the bourgeois class. What needs to be done is something quite different. One needs to investigate historically, and beginning from the lowest level, how mechanisms of power have been able to function' (1980: 100). In contrast to the liberal, individualist models, he argues: 'In fact, it is already one of the prime effects of power that certain bodies, certain gestures, certain discourses, certain desires, come to be identified and constituted as individuals. The individual, that is, is not the *vis-à-vis* of power; it is, I believe, one of its prime effects' (1980: 98). Rather than see power as located in a class or an individual, or in a state acting as if it were an individual, Foucault argues that power is 'never localised here or there', but rather 'employed and exercised through a net-like organisation' (1980: 98).

We can use five key ideas to sum up his critique of traditional approaches and his alternative theorization of power. Firstly, Foucault argues that power is not a substance that can be held by any one person or group. Rather, power is only ever exercised through relationships. Secondly, power relations are not external to other relations, so that we might treat certain economic relations as devoid of power. Rather, power is a feature of all relationships. In this sense, and thirdly, power does not operate in a top-down fashion, according to Foucault. Rather, it is fundamentally a bottom-up feature of social interaction. This has been taken to mean that Foucault has no place for power as domination, but in fact the claim he is defending is that power is not fundamentally a form of domination – even though it may occasionally take the form of domination. In light of these descriptions of power, it is not surprising that Foucault, fourthly, has no truck with the idea that power can be used cynically – by elites, for example. While he accepts that power relations have a strategic dimension in that they always serve some purpose, such strategic aims cannot be intentionally manipulated, because power is not a substance that can be deployed. As such, and perhaps most controversially, Foucault argued that there is no 'place' outside of power from which to resist it. Rather, power and resistance are always already mutually constitutive; there would be no way to resist if we were not already in a power relationship but, as resistance always means empowering oneself, one is simply reconstituting a relationship of power. As Foucault put it, though, power must never be viewed simply as a negative phenomenon: power 'incites' action every bit as much as it 'represses' action. We can make a connection between these aspects of power if we consider the ways in which, according to Foucault, power creates our sense of what counts as normal, and how the liberal democratic state is implicated in this process. In *Discipline and Punish* Foucault claims:

> Historically, the process by which the bourgeoisie became in the course of the eighteenth century the politically dominant class was masked by the establishment of an explicit, coded, and formally egalitarian juridical framework, made possible by the organisation of a parliamentary, representative regime. But the development and the generalisation of disciplinary mechanisms constituted the other, dark side of the processes. The general juridical form that guaranteed a system of rights that were egalitarian in principle was supported by these tiny everyday physical mechanisms, by all those systems of micro-power that are essentially non-egalitarian and asymmetrical that we call the disciplines. (1977: 222)

The aim of these disciplines was population control, or what Foucault calls bio-politics. Liberal governmentality (see Chapter 1) was, and continues to be, based on the nuances of disciplinary power as much as on the legitimate authority of the state. This dual aspect is captured by the idea of the norm: it is both that which justifies behaviour and that which people internalize as appropriate behaviour. It is, as Foucault says, 'a mixture of legality and nature, prescription and constitution, the norm' (1977: 304). Importantly, norms of both sorts require people to judge them, in terms of both their legitimacy and their effectiveness. Foucault therefore presents us with a vision of the liberal state as a state where judges of normality are everywhere: 'We are in the society of the teacher-judge, the doctor-judge, the educator-judge, the social worker-judge; it is on them that the universal reign of the normative is based; and each individual, wherever he may find himself, subjects to it his body, his gestures, his behaviour, his aptitudes, his achievements' (1977: 304). As he succinctly put it: 'The Enlightenment, which discovered the liberties, also invented the disciplines' (1977: 222).

Foucault's micro-physics of power relations turns around many of the presuppositions guiding other accounts of the relationship between the state and power. No longer is the state a political actor holding power over those who do not have it; no longer does the state organize the oppression of some people in the interests of others; no longer is the state a single coherent entity that stands above or apart from the political world; no longer is it the state that secures our liberties. Rather, the state may act as a focus for power relations, but only to the extent that it functions within a broader network of power relations; the state may dominate sections of society, but this reflects the distribution of power relations and is not a fundamental feature of the state itself; the state is a multi-faceted, complex assemblage of interlocking and interwoven power relations that extend within its borders and beyond its boundaries; the state disciplines individuals into behaving normally by creating and maintaining subtle and not-so-subtle forms of socialization which regulate social and political life as if 'from within'.

Inventive as Foucault's analysis is, it raises many questions, not the least of these being whether such a thesis can be normatively sustained. While Foucault's analyses of power claim to undermine the legitimacy of norms, they also appear to invoke norms, at least to the extent that Foucault appears to be embracing an emancipatory agenda (Taylor, 1985). If this is the case, then Foucault may suffer from what Habermas (1987) calls 'cryptonormativism': the surreptitious deployment of norms that are under-elaborated and poorly justified. If so, then perhaps we need to return to the heartlands of normative theory by enquiring into the value that many believe is central to political philosophy: justice.

CHAPTER 4

SOCIAL JUSTICE AND EQUALITY

We have discussed different ways in which government can be said to be authorized to rule over us in the name of protecting our liberties (Chapter 2) and how, in fact, such authorization is often manifest as the power of the state to oppress or discipline its citizens, threatening these very same liberties (Chapter 3). Maybe we need to ask a slightly different, albeit related, set of questions in order to get to the fundamental issues of political philosophy. One question that has good claim to be at the very centre of political philosophy is this: what would it mean for us all to be treated justly and equally? Of course, these days we tend to assume that justice demands equality (in some sense), but this is a relatively modern way of thinking about these concepts. It was not always assumed that justice and equality were connected. In order to understand why, it is useful to travel back to the beginning of Western political philosophy: to Plato's *The Republic*.

THE GOOD LIFE

The Republic is written as a dialogue about justice with Socrates as the major character. Immediately, though, we must be careful about what Plato might have meant by justice. The dialogue begins with a discussion about what it means 'to do the right thing', and it is generally accepted that the Greek word that we tend to translate as 'justice' had this much broader meaning. This explains why Socrates' interlocutors offer a range of competing accounts of justice that might seem a bit off the point to modern ears: they argue, for example, that justice is giving back what you've borrowed, giving a person his/her due, or doing whatever the strongest person desires. Nonetheless, the early part of the dialogue is taken up with Socrates exposing each of these responses to 'doing the right thing' variously as ill-defined, problematic and self-defeating. The general point that emerges from these opening sections is the important one that justice (in this broad sense) cannot be defined as being good only relative to something else, such as strength or personality. Rather, we must try to understand the good of justice in itself, without subordinating it to some other good. At this point, however, the dialogue takes a famous twist: Socrates argues that it is easier to understand the demands of justice if we consider justice within the *polis* rather than the individual, because it is 'easier to recognize' justice within the larger entity of the city-state than within a single individual (1974: 117). The upshot is that the book generally credited with being the first book of political philosophy only ventures into the nature of the just polity in order to answer the question 'what is the right thing for an individual to do?'; a question at the heart of moral (not necessarily political) philosophy. Consequently, the long-standing relationship between moral and political philosophy that defines the normative mainstream was initially established with a rather dubious methodological manoeuvre which deemed the life of the individual and the life of the collective to be analogous. Crucially, this analogy established an explicit hierarchy: the moral domain is deemed the more important because it serves as the foundation of the political.

Nonetheless, such intriguing beginnings hardly invalidate normative political philosophy, and whatever Plato's justification for turning to the life of the *polis* (more on this to come), we can still ask: what is a just city, according to Plato? In short, the answer is that it is one where everyone has found his or her correct role within society as a whole. Because we all have different talents, attributes and capacities, we need to find where our talents fit best within society. Plato argues that there are three main 'classes' within which everyone will find a place: the artisan class (the tradesmen, the producers, the commercial class and the like), the auxiliaries (essentially the military), and the guardians (the class of 'philosopher-rulers' who lead the *polis*). As one might expect from such a division of labour, the truly just city is one in which these classes are ordered hierarchically: the guardians rule, the auxiliaries support them in their rule by providing internal and external protection, and the artisans – the great majority of people – are the ruled. When all of this is properly arranged, the city will function like a living organism: a coherent whole working in harmony with itself, each person contributing their talents to the overall survival and maintenance of the well-ordered, good society.

Why should philosophers rule? Plato gives a variety of answers to this question, but the most famous is encapsulated in the analogy of the cave (1974: 316–25). He argues that the vast majority of people never contemplate the reality of things; it is as if the masses are living in a cave, staring at the walls, watching shadows cast by shapes from above flit before them, but never questioning how the shadows are produced. To contemporize the analogy, it is as if we spend our lives watching television and assume, without question, that everything we see on the screen is real. Philosophers, in contrast, try to establish the reality of things. In contemplating the reality of things, Plato argues, they come to know what things are really like, behind the shadows and the TV screen. According to Plato, the ultimate reality of any given thing is its *Form*; the Form of something is its essential nature, above and beyond the particular features of actual examples of the thing itself. For instance, there are many different kinds of chair (political philosophers, like all philosophers, love using chairs as examples – probably because they spend so much time sitting on them!), but there is something that they all share, a 'quality of chairness', which is the ideal Form of all chairs. For Plato, this ideal Form is not some mere abstraction; it is, in fact, the reality of the chair. It is only the philosophers who clamber to the lip of the cave – who, through contemplation, come to 'see' the nature of what is really casting the shadows – who are able to appreciate the Form of the chair. It is only such philosophers who can say that they *know* the nature of all chairs. Most of us, still trapped in the shadowy world of the cave, are only ever giving our *opinion* about the nature of a chair (typically, based on whatever we have seen before us 'on the walls of the cave'), because we have not contemplated its reality. Importantly, these claims about appearance and reality apply to concepts as well as things: so there is a Form of justice that must be the same for individuals as it is for city-states, just as there is a Form of the chair that must be the same for two-, three- or four-legged chairs. Indeed, as we read Plato's dialogue we realize that it is this theory of Forms that retrospectively legitimates, in his view, the controversial move from justice in the individual to justice in the *polis*: in both, the ideal of justice can be seen where each part – of an individual or a city – fulfils its role in establishing the good life for the whole: the person or *polis*.

What is the relationship between the Form of the chair and the Form of justice? For Plato, just as individuals and cities are ordered hierarchically, so too are Forms; after all, it would make little sense to argue that the idea of a chair was equal to the idea of justice. Given this, it is not surprising to find that there is a Form at the top of the hierarchy. All Forms, from those of objects to those of ideas like justice, are essentially expressions of the supreme form of 'the Good': to 'contemplate the Good' is the supreme task of the philosopher on his or her trip to the lip of the cave. This is what we would now call the paradigmatic version of *value-monism*: the claim that all values fit together harmoniously and do not conflict with each other, in this case because they all find their place within an overarching ideal of the Good life. A truly just society, therefore, is one in which everybody is able to fulfil their potential and develop their talents – as artisan, soldier or ruler, depending on one's talents – because to do so will bring the individual and the *polis* together as one harmonious expression of 'the Good life'.

VALUE-PLURALISM

If 'the Good life' means living in a well-ordered, hierarchical society where everyone is playing their own small part in realizing a greater moral-political vision, then it is not surprising that Plato's ideal polity does not sound as enticing to contemporary ears as it may have done to the people of ancient Greece. Indeed, it has become a cliché of political philosophy to associate Plato's vision with the terrible dictatorships of the early twentieth century; a cliché that has its roots in Karl Popper's (1966) caricature of Plato's ideas in his book *The Open Society and Its Enemies*. But even if Popper overplayed the similarities between Plato's hierarchical Republic, Nazi Germany and Stalinist Russia, the notion that all our values can fit harmoniously into one overarching vision is not something that many modern political philosophers now accept. Indeed, one of the central features of modern (as opposed to classical) political philosophy is that it tends to be based on the presumption of *value-pluralism* (as opposed to value-monism). Although the roots of value-pluralism run deep in the canon of Western political thought, one of the most influential exponents of this idea was (not coincidentally, given the Cold War overtones) a contemporary of Popper: namely, the essayist and historian of ideas, Isaiah Berlin. According to Berlin:

The world that we encounter in ordinary experience is one in which we are faced with choices between ends equally ultimate, and claims equally absolute, the realization of some of which must inevitably involve the sacrifice of others. Indeed it is because this is their situation that men place such immense value upon the freedom to choose; for if they had assurance that in some perfect state, realizable by men on earth, no ends pursued by them would ever be in conflict, the necessity and the agony of choice would disappear, and with it the central importance of the freedom to choose. (1969: 168)

Value-pluralism, for Berlin, means there are a considerable, though not infinite, number of 'supreme values' that are in *conflict* with each other – incapable of being reconciled – and are in principle *incommensurable*, or incapable of being measured by the same standard. This means that any attempt to bring the 'supreme values' into harmony, by ordering them in relation to 'the Good' for example, will flounder. John Gray, a political philosopher continuing Berlin's work on value-pluralism and liberalism, puts it like this: '[E]thical life contains conflicts of values that are rationally undecidable, [and] that is a truth we must accept – not something we should seek to tidy away for the sake of theoretical consistency' (2000: 35). Indeed, the search for consistency in ethical life – the idea that a consistent ethical outlook is better than an inconsistent one – is denied by Gray: inconsistency can be truer to the demands of ethical life, since the tragic demands of having to choose between incompatible values in different contexts means that we do not make the same choice each time.

Recalling the definition of value-pluralism, the 'not an infinite number' rubric is important because it differentiates value-pluralism from value-relativism and value-subjectivism. Both Berlin and Gray insist that there are supreme values, such that many other values which are not supreme must be subordinate to them, and that these supreme values are few in number: 'to claim that some values are incommensurate does not mean that all values are equally valid' (Gray, 2000: 41). Berlin talks of a 'horizon of human values', to capture the plurality he has in mind. Gray distinguishes between forms of relativism (which assume an irreducible plurality of 'world-views') and subjectivism (which treat our values as expressions of our personal preferences) from value-pluralism on the basis that pluralism, unlike the other options, demands that judgements are made and assumes that we can judge between the supreme values, but also assumes that we can never *rationally* resolve any disagreements that result from these judgements. This is a description of the moral universe that many find intuitively appealing. However, it does raise some potentially difficult issues when one thinks through the political consequences. Gray (2000) admits, for example, that there are many difficulties with Berlin's value-pluralism, or more specifically with the way that Berlin draws political implications from this concept. Berlin tended to assume that value-pluralism could only be protected by appeal to negative liberty – freedom from interference (see Chapter 2) – but this, according to Gray, places the value of liberty, in its negative form at least, above other values, thereby contradicting the pluralism which it is supposed to defend. Berlin is to be applauded for recognizing that values can be *internally* plural – that there can be *two* concepts of liberty – but he retreats to the practice of 'rationalizing' liberalism by arguing that negative liberty must be given special status in order for value-pluralism to flourish.

All this poses a problem for Gray: how can he defend the idea of liberalism on the basis of value-pluralism if prioritizing negative liberty is ruled out? The solution, for Gray, is what he calls a view of liberal toleration. For Gray, a truly liberal version of toleration, which recognizes the intrinsically plural nature of the moral sphere, is one that simply aims to establish terms of peace; terms that are not in need of rational justification and that do not presume a strong sense of consensus. 'Liberalism's future,' he says, 'lies in turning its face away from the ideal of rational consensus and looking instead to *modus Vivendi*' (2000: 105), where 'modus Vivendi' is to be understood as a practical compromise. By way of example, he argues that thinking of human rights as 'immutable truths', or as 'moral absolutes', or as guarantors of or prerequisites for a liberal form of global governance, is not only mistaken but dangerous. Rights are entirely conventional, thereby changeable in different historical and cultural contexts. That they will come into conflict is inevitable for Gray (and he notes, with some justification, that rights-based discourse is a staple part of the diet that sustains most long-standing conflicts), but to see this conflict as resolvable through reasonable discourse is simply to neglect the plurality of incommensurable values that the very idea of rights contains within itself. He says:

There can be no definitive list of human rights. Rights are not theorems that fall out of theories of law or ethics. They are judgements about human interests whose content shifts over time as threats to human interests change. When we ask which rights are universal, we are not inquiring after a truth that exists already. We are asking a question that demands a practical decision: which human interests warrant universal protection? (2000: 113)

But is the idea of *modus Vivendi* sustainable? Gray argues that the aim of peaceful co-existence is not a good in itself, not a good that can be shown to be prior to or higher than all other values; rather, it is a contingent good that 'nearly all' ways of life presuppose (peaceful co-existence is seen as necessary to the pursuit of almost any way of life). But as a contingent good, what of those ways of life that do not support peaceful co-existence? Gray says they are rare if not non-existent, on the grounds that ways of life emerge in response to human interests and these are sufficiently common as well as sufficiently diverse to give support to the idea of peaceful co-existence.

All of which, it must be said, seems to lead Gray into difficulty verging on confusion. First, the idea of practical compromise appears to be premised on a theoretical rationalization of human interests that may be said to imply a number of claims about human goods. Secondly, to define rights as merely conventional robs them of any force they might have in helping the oppressed of different cultures (more on the complications of this in Chapter 6). Third, it seems plausible to assume (and we can look around the world for evidence of this) that human interests can coalesce around the unequal treatment of some of the members of a group – women, for example. In such cases, conventional 'terms of peace' have been worked out, but unfair and unequal treatment of individuals continues. Is it not the task of political philosophers to show why such unequal treatment is morally wrong, from a rational point of view? Such questions point us back to a theory of justice and equality, but one which does not assume that justice is found in the contemplation of a single vision of the good life.

JUSTICE AS FAIRNESS

In 1971 (1972 in the UK) the publication of John Rawls' *A Theory of Justice* transformed political philosophy by bringing the question of justice back into the centre of the discipline. After centuries of neglect because of its association with outdated visions of the good life, Rawls developed a theory aimed at showing how a just society could be achieved *given* that there are many, equally reasonable, versions of the good life. Rawls' aim was to theorize a just solution to the problem of how we get along with each other in light of this diversity of views about the good life – without, of course, simply imposing one such view at the expense of the others. Just to be clear though, and given the millennia that separate them, it wasn't the value-monism of Plato that Rawls was particularly concerned to counter. Rather, the more contemporary version of value-monism which had assumed a certain dominant place in moral and political philosophy of the late nineteenth and early twentieth centuries was utilitarianism; in particular, the English utilitarian tradition of Jeremy Bentham, John Stuart Mill and Henry Sidgwick. Rawls' own characterization of it was this: the main idea of utilitarianism is that 'society is rightly ordered, and therefore just, when its major institutions are arranged so as to achieve the greatest net balance of satisfaction summed over all the individuals belonging to it' (1972: 22). This is a rather more technical version of 'the greatest happiness for the greatest number' principle that underpins utilitarianism. As is well known, though, the utilitarian approach to society does not, in itself, guarantee the individual liberties of the members of a polity. It is possible that if the utility principle is applied strictly and straightforwardly, the liberty of one or some could be sacrificed for the overall happiness of the majority. For example, if there were an overall increase in happiness following the incarceration of homosexuals then the utility principle would suggest that this would be the right course of action. It appears to allow, therefore, for (possibly quite heinous) offences against individual liberties. Rawls gives his summary verdict on the issue as follows: 'Justice denies that the loss of freedom for some is made right by a greater good shared by others' (1972: 28). Rawls, in brief, treats the problem of liberty as insurmountable within a utilitarian approach: the liberty of everybody must be paramount, and can never be sacrificed for the happiness of oneself or other individuals. In place of utilitarianism, Rawls revitalizes the idea of social contract theory (see Chapter 2) in order to give as strong a foundation as possible to his defence of the unassailable rights of the individual. In contrast to earlier contract thinkers, however, Rawls argues that the basic task of a social contract is not merely to establish the nature and limits of political authority but to create principles of justice that will require the political authority to be *fair* to all. Nonetheless, like other social contract thinkers, Rawls views society as:

> a more or less self-sufficient association of persons who in their relations to one another recognise certain rules of conduct as binding and who for the most part act in accordance with them . . . these rules specify a system of cooperation designed to advance the good of those taking part in it. (1972: 4)

This is a typically liberal view of society as a bond between individuals established in order to serve the interests of the individuals themselves. Just to reiterate, therefore, this means that Rawls' turn to the idea of justice is not to be understood as a return to the classical Platonic concern with justice in which justice requires the realization of a single vision of the good life. Rather, according to Rawls, 'on the contract view the grounds of liberty are completely separate from existing preferences . . . the indeterminacy in the full theory of the good is no cause for objection' (1972: 450). In other words, the fact that we do not share a single sense of what would constitute 'the Good life' does not invalidate the pursuit of justice. It merely changes the nature of the justice that we seek. In fact, Rawls calls his modern, liberal view of justice 'justice as fairness'. Justice, therefore, has a particular meaning and is *not* co-extensive with morality. It is 'social justice' that Rawls is concerned with:

> For us the primary subject of justice is the basic structure of society, or more exactly, the way in which the major social institutions distribute fundamental rights and duties and determine the division of advantages from social cooperation. By major institutions I understand the political constitution and the principal economic and social arrangements. (1972: 7)

The aim is to find a series of fundamental principles that will bring about the *fair* distribution of these rights, duties and advantages. It is this guiding intuition that leads Rawls to say that 'justice is the first virtue of social institutions, as truth is of systems of thought' (1972: 3). Indeed, even if people 'hold different conceptions of justice', argues Rawls, they can 'still agree that institutions are just when no arbitrary distinctions are made between persons in the assigning of basic rights and duties and when the rules determine a proper balance between competing claims to the advantages of social life' (1972: 5). But how is a fair distribution to be found? In short, Rawls argues that a fair procedure for finding the principles will result in fair principles: a fair starting point plus a fair process will equal a fair outcome:

> The guiding idea is that the principles of justice for the basic structure of society are the object of the original agreement. They are the principles that free and rational persons concerned to further their own interests would accept in an initial position of equality as defining the fundamental terms of their association. (1972: 11)

So if we agree to a fair basic structure as part of an original contract, then all other constitutional, legislative and judicial decisions would be regulated by the terms of the original agreement and we would have a just social order. But this raises many questions: How can we create a fair original agreement? What is an initial position of equality? What principles would emerge?

Social contract theory fell out of favour in political thought largely as a result of Bentham's (1988) robust rhetoric regarding the fallacy of basing political authority on a 'fictional' agreement that clearly never really took place. Although the actual historical fact of a founding social contract is unnecessary to contract theory (see Chapter 2), Rawls construes the 'original agreement' he envisages as explicitly, unequivocally *hypothetical* in order to avoid any confusion. It is a thought-experiment aimed at clarifying our moral intuitions which uses contract theory as a method or procedure for deriving principles of justice, a procedure that he feels does not substantively define the nature of any principles that would emerge.

On what basis would any agreement regarding principles of justice need to rest for it to be a fair agreement? One element is to have a situation of initial fairness; Rawls' calls this the 'original position'. The original position, for all that it sounds like the first chapter of the *Karma Sutra*, is in fact Rawls' characterization of a situation in which individuals looking to reach an agreement about how to get on with each other fairly could be thought to be equals. If the people deciding on the just distribution of the 'rights, duties and advantages of social cooperation' are not equals, then the agreement reached is hardly likely to be fair for every member of society. But would the individuals in the original position not be subject to all sorts of factors that might distort the process of reaching agreement? The wealth, power, charisma, intelligence, class, race or simple good fortune of some might be used to create a social order that would favour them. It is with such concerns in mind that Rawls elaborates upon the thought-experiment by imagining how individuals would reason in the original position if they were behind a 'veil of ignorance'. The veil of ignorance is a theoretical device for depriving individuals of a range of knowledge that might jeopardize the fairness of the original position. Behind the 'veil of ignorance'

[n]o one knows his place in society, his class position or social status, nor does anyone know his fortune in the distribution of natural assets and abilities, his intelligence, strength and the like . . . the parties do not know their conceptions of the good . . . This ensures that no one is advantaged or disadvantaged by the outcome of natural chance or contingency of social circumstances. Since all are similarly situated and no one is able to design principles to favour his particular condition, the principles of justice are the result of a fair agreement. (1972: 11)

The device of the veil of ignorance provides the moral basis of the original position, the fair starting point from which a founding agreement can be constructed. Because, hypothetically, we do not know what our 'place' in the new society will be – whether or not we will be rich, poor, in the majority or one of the minorities, able-bodied or disabled, articulate or not, and so on – Rawls argues that the agreement we reach in the original position, behind the veil of ignorance, will necessarily be an agreement that secures justice for all in society. He asserts that as the individuals in the original position do not know their place in the social order then they will reason as follows: all principles that are agreed must be to the benefit of those less well situated in society – in case I am one of them! This is called the *maximin* approach to reasoning: all parties to the original agreement will seek to maximize the interests of the worst-off group, that is, to *maximize the minimum* outcome. In other words, reasoning from within the original position, behind the veil of ignorance, is a hypothetical device for establishing what would be a fair distribution of the 'rights, duties and advantages' that result from our cooperation in society.

Before presenting the principles that, according to Rawls, the individuals would all agree to, it is necessary for the sake of clarity to present some other features of the original position that (mainly) serve to explain the motivations at work in it. Rawls notes that each imaginary individual in the original position must be aware that it is a 'device of representation'. Each contractor must know that they 'represent' someone 'in the real world', so to speak, in order to avoid contractors formulating principles based on fantastical notions (for example, 'If I am a unicorn then unicorns must have rights'). Furthermore, and crucially, each contractor is denied access to their own particular conception of the good – they do not know if they value the quiet life, the life of social engagement, the religious life, the pursuit of knowledge, family attachments, or whatever – because this is a way of ensuring that the principles reflect the plurality of views on the good life that characterizes modernity. That said, each of Rawls' imaginary contractors is presumed to value more rather than fewer 'primary goods'. These are the means to achieve a variety of different ends, which are 'rights and liberties, powers and opportunities, income and wealth' (1972: 62) and the bases of self-respect (1972: 440). The primary goods are 'primary' precisely because without them one could not pursue the kind of life one wants to pursue. It is these primary goods that are the subject of the principles that emerge. Moreover, each contractor is assumed to be both rationally motivated (wanting to maximize their own position within society) and reasonable (aware of the interests of other people). This entails that the contractors are non-envious, disinterested, and ready to abide by the principles they have freely chosen. Lastly, the contractors also know that they will live within a society where the circumstances of justice prevail. Rawls divides these into objective circumstances such as moderate scarcity, and subjective circumstances such as competing conceptions of the good. This ensures that the reasoning of the individuals in the original position is not distorted by assumptions such as the never-ending provision of resources.

Equally, it is important that the individuals in the original position have some limited sense of the task in hand. Rawls therefore restricts the scope of justice to the national (or, as he confusingly refers to it, the 'domestic') level of distributive justice, thereby excluding what he calls local (for example, in the family) or global (as in the relation between states) questions of justice. With regard to this domestic level, Rawls builds into his contractors' thoughts the knowledge that the principles of justice they create will apply to a 'closed' society, by which he means that it will be ordered around a coercive state. The implication of this is that the contractors would not be able to simply leave once the veil has been lifted, as this would create the possibility of their agreeing to unjust principles – which is not to say that emigration could not be countenanced within the framework of the principles themselves, once the principles of a just basic structure had been established. Furthermore, Rawls assumes that the society to which the principles apply will be 'well-ordered'. That is, it will be a society designed to advance the principles arrived at – coercively, if necessary.

Given these motivational assumptions and limitations of task, Rawls argues that individuals in a fair original position, behind a veil of ignorance to ensure that biases are removed, would reason their way to agreeing on what he calls the 'general conception of justice': 'All social values – liberty and opportunity, income and wealth and the bases of self-respect – are to be distributed equally unless an unequal distribution of any, or all, of these values is to everyone's advantage' (1972: 62). This can be presented in a particular 'special conception' of justice with two principles (this version is from a later work, *Justice as Fairness: A Restatement* which is rather clearer than the versions to be found in *A Theory of Justice*):

First: 'each person has the same indefeasible claim to a fully adequate scheme of equal basic liberties, which scheme is compatible with the same scheme of liberties for all.'
Second: 'social and economic inequalities are to satisfy two conditions: (a) that they are to be attached to offices and positions open to all under conditions of fair equality of opportunity; and (b) that they are to be to the greatest benefit of the least advantaged members of society (the difference principle). (2001: 42–3)

The first principle establishes *equal basic liberties* for all regardless of personal advantages such as wealth, power and intelligence. The second principle provides two conditions that *legitimate inequality*. Rawls adds that it would be irrational in the original position to suppose that one might sacrifice one's basic liberties for economic or social gain, in which case the first principle has priority over the second. Basic liberties can only be sacrificed for the sake of liberty itself. Moreover, he argues that it would be irrational to agree to the sacrifice of equality of opportunity for economic inequality (for example, we wouldn't give up the chance of equal employment rights in the hope that some of us in the original position might turn out to have more money than others). Rawls refers to the priority of the first over the second principle, and of 2(a) over 2(b), as the lexical ordering of the principles of justice.

Why should we accept Rawls' account of the original position and the principles that, he argues, follow from it? How do we know that the principles are really fair? Rawls argues that the original position and the veil of ignorance are merely hypothetical devices for clarifying our presuppositions about what constitutes a fair starting point, procedure and outcome. We can see this by considering *unfair* starting points, procedures and outcomes when it comes to defining principles of justice. The veil of ignorance, in particular, means that we will make morally justifiable decisions by excluding from our deliberations aspects of our status, identity, and so on that are 'arbitrary from a moral point of view' (1972: 14). However, thinking about a just distribution of rights, duties and advantages from such an explicitly hypothetical point of view may tell us little about the real conditions necessary for a fair and just society. For Rawls, this criticism misses the point (although we will see a more developed version of this concern in the last section of this chapter) because the aim of the thought-experiment is to enable us to reflect more deeply on our intuitions, and to stimulate us into thinking about how the principles agreed under such ideal conditions can be brought into a 'reflective equilibrium' with the moral intuitions that guide our everyday lives.

Drawing these threads together, we can say that for Rawls, a liberal society is one in which all individuals are treated as ends in themselves (not as elements in a utilitarian calculation), and a just social order is one in which the right balance of liberty and equality is enshrined in the basic structure of that society. Ensuring this balance means that basic liberties must be equally protected, and that social and economic inequality is only legitimate when it benefits the worst-off in society. But has Rawls tipped the scales of justice too far in favour of equality, and put liberty in jeopardy? This was the view of Robert Nozick, whose *Anarchy State and Utopia* was the first of a series of famous and influential responses to Rawls' egalitarian approach to social justice from across the political-philosophical spectrum.

JUSTICE AS ENTITLEMENT

Rawls' redistributive principle – *the difference principle* – assumes that one's position in society is not one's own fault, and that an individual should not be arbitrarily disadvantaged by something that is not his/her own fault (hence the idea that all decisions about how to share out the advantages of society should aim to benefit the worst-off). The theory does not mention the need for redistribution, primarily the redistribution of wealth that people already own. Such redistribution would involve taking something that belongs to someone and giving it to someone else. It seems justified to say, with Nozick, that this violates the freedom of individuals to dispose of their wealth on whatever grounds they want and not on the basis of some spurious goal-driven notion of 'a better, more equal, society'.

Nozick develops an imaginary example that he thinks captures the intuition precisely. We may imagine a society with an equal distribution of wealth (distribution 1). Into this society we place a famous basketball player – Wilt Chamberlain – who, because of his great skill on the court, is in huge demand. Knowing the demand he is generating, Wilt signs a contract with his basketball team that increases the price of each ticket by 25 cents on condition that this money goes directly to him. Over the season Wilt makes a huge amount of money, say $250,000 on top of his usual salary. We now have a second distribution of wealth (distribution 2) that is far from equal. How, asks Nozick, 'can anyone else complain on grounds of justice? . . . [T]here is nothing that anyone has that anyone else has a claim of justice against' (1974: 161). In order to maintain the original equal distribution people would have to be prohibited from spending their own 25 cents. Or, in order to minimize the difference between Wilt and everyone else, there would have to be a massive redistribution of the money that people have freely given to Wilt. Redistribution in this way would require violating individual liberty, argues Nozick. Typically, the redistributive method would be taxation, but this means that part of our hard-earned money would be taken by the state to redistribute for the sake of a 'social good' such as a more equal society. Importantly, for Nozick, this is not necessarily what an individual may think of as 'a good'. In fact, taxation as a means of redistribution means that part of an individual's working day is not being spent for him/herself, but for the 'social good' according to the state's definition. Nozick concludes that 'Taxation of earnings from labour is on a par with forced labour' (1974: 169).

In general, argues Nozick, 'end-result principles of justice' (those that justify a particular distribution of resources, such as an equal distribution, as just) and 'historical but patterned principles of justice' (those that take the form 'from each according to X, to each according to Y') will lead to 'continuous interference with people's lives' (1974: 163). They will, therefore, result in the violation of an individual's right to dispose of his or her own wealth in pursuit of whatever goals the individual values in life – such as watching a skilful basketball player. Nozick concludes that 'liberty upsets patterns' and that 'any distributional pattern with any egalitarian component is overturnable by the voluntary actions of individual persons over time' (1974: 164).

In place of Rawls' distributive approach to what makes a just society, Nozick offers a Lockean entitlement theory that he argues is an historical but *unpatterned* theory of justice. In short, whereas distributive approaches to justice focus on 'who gets what?', entitlement approaches focus on the question 'are you entitled to what you have?'. For Nozick, a 'distribution is just if everyone is *entitled* to the holdings they possess under the distribution' (1974: 151). This raises two issues: (a) what constitutes the just *transfer* of goods and wealth, and (b) what legitimates the just *acquisition* of goods and wealth? A just transfer of wealth is simply one that was freely given and received: by gift, bequest or charity donation; or, of course, by free-market transaction. When it comes to property acquisition, Nozick is a thorough-going Lockean (see Chapter 2): property or wealth can be acquired from the common stock as long as 'enough and as good' is left for others. Interestingly, Nozick interprets this to mean that the acquisition of property must not worsen the situation of others (an intuition not that far away from Rawls') but he also argues that the operation of the capitalist free market based on the ownership of private property benefits everyone, as everyone would be worse off if property rights were not recognized. Nozick argues, therefore, that the free market does not make anyone worse off. Of course, sometimes wealth is distributed in unjust ways (by fraud and theft, for example) and Nozick recognizes that there must be a principle of *rectification* to accompany the principles of just transfer and just acquisition. Rectification simply means rectifying an unjust transfer or acquisition, and we will know what to rectify and how by simply asking: what would the distribution of wealth be if the unjust transfer or acquisition had not taken place?

But this alerts us to some problems with Nozick's entitlement theory. Beginning with the principle of rectification, it becomes difficult to conceive of how this would work almost as soon as one tries to apply it. How, for example, are we to sort out difficult cases such as whether or not the vast majority of property held in the USA was unjustly acquired or transferred from the native peoples? Can we establish what the distribution would be like if there had been no unjust transfers or acquisitions? Nozick is oblique on this point, in effect suggesting that such issues will have to be worked out by way of one-off decisions to which all would agree. The deeper issue hiding behind this one, however, is that the nature of property ownership is underdeveloped in Nozick's entitlement approach. He assumes that an already formed and rational individual has complete ownership of his or her property. But his account neglects to mention that any individual requires a social apparatus of family, education, health services and the like in order to get to the stage of owning property at all. In which case, it seems overly simplistic to say that any given individual simply owns everything they have: shouldn't the property also be owned, in part at least, by all those who have contributed to the individual's capacity for ownership? This rhetorical question points to perhaps the deepest issue of all that Nozick's stark individualism raises: is it really correct to think of ourselves as self-owners, as individuals who own our own selves? The strict separation of persons this implies is counter-intuitive once we consider the overlapping and intertwined lives we lead as real people embroiled in real relationships which reach deeper than legal contracts and free market transactions. Perhaps we need to tip the balance of justice back in favour of equality. But what would this require if we think about justice for women?

CARE AND JUSTICE

The differences between men and women which I describe centre on a tendency for women and men to make different relational errors – for men to think that if they know themselves, following

Socrates' dictum, they will also know women, and for women to think that if they only know others, they will come to know themselves. Thus men and women tacitly collude in not voicing women's experiences, and build relationships around a silence that is maintained by men's not knowing their disconnection from women and women's not knowing their dissociation from themselves. Much talk about relationships and about love carefully conceals these truths. (Gilligan, 1993: xx)

The work of Carol Gilligan has proved very influential in framing the debates that have come to be known as the sameness/difference debates within feminism, and the care vs justice debates in political theory. What is Gilligan's core idea? She argues that there are empirically verifiable differences between the way women and men think about our relationships with each other, particularly with regard to how women and men evaluate these relationships. In a nutshell, Gilligan argues that men emphasize individualism, rights and justice (men emphasize *moral* systems, which are deemed to be neutral and universal), while women tend to emphasize relationality, duty and care (women therefore emphasize *ethical* systems, which are value-laden and contextual). The implication that many have drawn from this is that women have a different way of evaluating relationships from men, and this must be recognized and respected in the construction of our social and political arrangements. But before going into more detail on the care vs justice debate, it is useful to look at the background to Gilligan's work. What follows is a significantly abridged version of one of the most notorious and contested theories of modern thought. For those who wish to pursue the theory in more depth, Freud's essays 'The ego and the id' and 'The dissolution of the Oedipus complex' are the classic statements; both are available in Gay (1995).

At the core of classic Freudian psychoanalysis is the Oedipus complex, a narrative of familial relations that is supposed to account for the ways in which children develop a sense of their own ego, or self. For Freud, young boys initially love their mother but in doing so experience (or imagine they experience) the jealous rage of their father, who seeks to deny the boy access to the mother. Such initial stirrings are buried during a period of latency, only to re-emerge as the boy comes to realize his sexuality in puberty. As this maturation occurs, the father threatens (or the adolescent boy imagines that the father is threatening) to 'castrate' him (not literally!) unless he stops loving his, the boy's, mother. A series of choices emerge for the young boy at this stage but typically the boy realizes the power of the father and aligns with it, separating from the mother and identifying with the 'law of the father'. What of young girls? For Freud, the young girl, over a similar period of time as the boy, is also forced by the father (or imagines she is) to separate from the mother, but as there is no penis to threaten with castration, the girl conjectures that she is already castrated (the psychological war has already been lost) and she turns this realization against her mother, as it was clearly her mother who brought her into the world without the phallic power necessary to survive within it. She now, according to Freud, loves her father and hates her mother, but because she knows that she can never identify with the father completely (because she has no penis/phallus) then she never completely resolves the identity crisis brought about by (incomplete) separation from her mother.

As Freud extrapolated his ideas beyond family life (his later work, in particular, tackles the psychological underpinnings of society and civilization) he came to consider the unresolved castration of the young girl as the root of gender differences in the way men and women relate to morality. Freud concluded that women 'show less sense of justice than men, that they are less ready to submit to the great exigencies of life, that they are more often influenced in their judgements by feelings of affection or hostility' (Freud, quoted in Gilligan, 1993: 7). Clearly, Freud viewed these female traits as deficiencies; in his view, women simply failed to live up to the full identity which is acquired by men as a result of their primordial identification with the law of the father. Women, as de Beauvoir would say, are undoubtedly treated as the 'second sex', from a psychoanalytical point of view.

For Gilligan, however, the turning point in her understanding of Freudian theory was her reading of work by the psychoanalytical feminist, Nancy Chodorow. For Gilligan, Chodorow's work took the basic Freudian distinction between the sexes, exposed the male-centeredness of its analysis, and in turn removed the hierarchy based on the different way in which women construct relationships. In her own summary of Chodorow's analysis she says:

> Consequently, relationships, and particularly issues of dependency, are experienced differently by women and men. For boys and men, separation and individuation are critically tied to gender identity

since separation from the mother is essential for the development of masculinity. For girls and women, issues of femininity or feminine identity do not depend upon the achievement of separation from the mother or on the progress of individuation . . . males tend to have difficulty with relationships, while females tend to have problems with individuation. (1993: 8)

This psychoanalytical background provides the meta-theoretical framework for Gilligan's own work in empirically oriented developmental psychology. But to see the importance of her contribution to this field, we need to mention briefly the approach of her mentor, Lawrence Kohlberg. Kohlberg tried to understand the origins and development of moral thinking within individuals. He developed, by way of Kant's moral philosophy and Piaget's work on child development, a research programme that investigated underlying principles of moral engagement. He concluded that moral development can be said to correlate to three broad stages of moral thinking (each with two parts, but we need not pursue these): pre-conventional, conventional and post-conventional. The last was deemed the highest form, such that a post-conventional moral thinker is one who initially deals with competing perspectives impartially, objectively and with due process, and who then ultimately recognizes that universal moral principles are principles of justice – thereby 'internalizing' within himself legal impartiality and moral universality.

As Gilligan points out: 'In this version of moral development, however, the conception of maturity is derived from the study of men's lives and reflects the importance of individuation in their development' (1993: 18). It is no surprise that women fare very badly on this measure of moral development, because (as is so often the case) women are being judged by male standards that fail to express a women's perspective. Is it possible, Gilligan considers, that women speak 'in a different voice' when women speak morally? To answer this question she carried out her own studies into the moral development of men and women, the results of which form the body of her book.

When one begins with the study of women and derives developmental constructs from their lives, the outline of a moral conception different from that described by Freud, Piaget or Kohlberg begins to emerge and informs a different description of development.

In this conception, the moral problem arises from conflicting responsibilities rather than from competing rights and requires for its resolution a mode of thinking that is contextual and narrative rather than formal and abstract. This conception of morality as concerned with the activity of care centers moral development around the understanding of responsibility and relationships, just as the conception of morality as fairness ties moral development to the understanding of rights and rules. (1993: 19)

What are the implications of this for political philosophy? As we have seen, political thought arguably begins with the Platonic question 'what is justice?'. While political theory has veered away from this defining question at key moments in its history, the publication of Rawls' *A Theory of Justice* has almost single-handedly brought justice back centre-stage; for Rawls, after all, 'justice is the first virtue of social institutions'. Interestingly, Rawls engages briefly with Kohlberg's work towards the end of *A Theory of Justice*, cautiously adopting and adapting elements of it (1972: 461–2). Jürgen Habermas, another central figure in contemporary political theory (see Chapters 5 and 6), also applies Kohlberg's stages of individual moral development to a reconstructed version of historical materialism: Habermas talks of 'societies' being at pre-conventional, conventional and post-conventional stages of moral development. Given this context, Gilligan's insights seem very relevant for political philosophy.

If one broadly accepts Gilligan's conclusions then there are three different ways of 'incorporating' her work into political philosophy. Firstly, it could be argued that the idea of justice is inherently masculine. A political theory that genuinely gives women a voice will not have 'what is justice?' as its guiding question. Political philosophy, it could be argued, must be re-conceptualized in its entirety because justice is antithetical to care. Audre Lorde's (1983) remark that 'one will never dismantle the master's house with the master's tools' gives powerful poetic expression to this over-arching critique of the political-philosophical canon. That said, there is a great danger in pursuing this line because the idea of 'justice for women', as feminists like Martha Nussbaum (1999) have pointed out, has been a corner-stone of feminist theory and practice that few would deny has promoted the advancement of women. So, secondly, it could be argued that the ethic of care and the morality of justice frameworks are different ways of evaluating social and political life that could co-exist in our deeply value-pluralist world. Perhaps women's voices can be heard as different yet equal voices within the political world? One can view Seyla Benhabib's (1987) approach to social and political theory within this broad perspective. However, there remains the problem of what to do when these conflict, as they will. If care and justice condition different responses to tricky relationship issues, which will 'win out' in any given circumstance, and why? Or do we have to accept that the world of values is messy, not susceptible to rational solutions, and the complex decisions we have to make are simply an irremovable aspect of that world? A third option, however, is to argue that the idea of justice has been constructed across the millennia in a masculine way but that it can be *reconstructed* to accommodate an ethic of care. Perhaps a fuller and richer understanding of justice could include within it the ethic of care? Susan Moller Okin (1989) is notable in this regard as a Rawlsian liberal feminist who has argued that Rawls' theory of justice does provide for caring and sympathetic relationships within the bounds of the original position. But there is a danger here: does this not negate Gilligan's insights by ultimately drowning out women's voices once again? What about Gilligan, whose work, after all, kicked off this debate? In truth, Gilligan is keen not to get involved in these debates, though she does suggest that there seems to be the possibility of a more balanced grasp of both care and justice that both sexes can reach as they 'mature' (1993: Chapter 6). However, it is not clear why this development might come about, or what its full implications would be.

It is clear, though, that Gilligan's work has caused great controversy, not least within feminist circles:

> The women's morality Gilligan discovers cannot be morality 'in a different voice'. It can only be morality in the feminine voice, in a higher register. Women are said to value care. Perhaps women value care because men have valued women according to the care they give. Women are said to think in relational terms. Perhaps women think in relational terms because women's social existence is defined in relation to men. The liberal idealism of these works is revealed in the ways they do not take social determination and the realities of power seriously enough. (MacKinnon, 1989: 51–2)

MacKinnon does not see Gilligan's work as a potential way of understanding, or even glimpsing, what a non-patriarchal society might be like. Rather she sees Gilligan's work as simply mirroring the very patriarchal construction of women that she says must be overcome. Indeed, MacKinnon argues that Gilligan's work could be a hindrance to the project of women's emancipation because it makes women affirm the identity that has been constructed for them by men. Are we faced with a stark dichotomy? *Either*: Gilligan, the gender-sensitive researcher who has given women access to their ethical voice, one that has been denied them by generations of moral thinkers, and who has therefore opened up the possibility of thinking 'outside the patriarchal box' when it comes to our political life and institutions. *Or*: Gilligan, the female dupe of the patriarchal structure who merely mirrors back to women what men want of women, in such a way that women are once again silenced – but even more dangerously, since this is a silence they are asked to be complicit with and to celebrate.

THE RETURN OF THE GOOD

Such stark dichotomies may be a permanent feature of political philosophy or they may be symptomatic of a deeper malaise, a malaise at the heart of modern liberal democracies brought about by the loss of communal bonds. For all that the bourgeois revolutions of early modern European and American history led to the overthrow of arbitrary authority imposed from above, it may be that the emphasis on individual freedoms has slowly but surely eroded our sense of togetherness. If so, then the task of political philosophy may not be to articulate a just accommodation between competing individuals, but rather to remind people of the deep-seated commonalities that underpin their sense of themselves as belonging to a community. These themes are given powerful expression in the body of work known as communitarianism. I will briefly introduce two communitarians, Michael Sandel and Charles Taylor, by presenting their work as a response to Rawls'.

Sandel (1984) offers a wide array of arguments to challenge the individualist assumptions behind Rawls' theory of 'justice as fairness'. Sandel begins by reconstructing the standard 'liberal vision'. It is, he says, one which gives 'priority to the right over the good', which means that liberals do not believe in a single version of the good life, but rather they wish to secure as large an area of personal freedom, through a series of rights, in order to allow individuals to pursue their own conception of the good (without infringing the freedom of others). Individual rights, therefore, must not be sacrificed for the greater good, and our social and political institutions must be constructed so as to recognize reasonable pluralism. Sandel links this liberal vision to the Kantian concept of the (transcendental) subject that is prior to experience; he argues that it is a view of the self that legitimates the claim that 'the right is prior to the good', which means that it results in a higher value being placed on an individual's right to pursue their own version of the good life than on any idea of the common good. He goes on to argue that Rawls' original position serves to enrich this Kantian heritage in that it explicitly formulates an account of an *unencumbered* self: a 'self understood as prior to and independent of purposes and ends' (1984: 86). The upshot for Rawls, according to Sandel, is initially quite a liberating sense of liberalism: as Rawls states, we are 'self-originating sources of valid claims'. But Sandel expresses doubts: 'This is an exhilarating vision . . . But is it true?' (1984: 87).

He tackles this question by arguing that Rawls' difference principle may be premised on a view of the unencumbered self, but it presupposes a view of the self as encumbered specifically by 'antecedent obligations that would undercut the priority of right' (1984: 90). His argument is this: as an unencumbered self I do not deserve the benefits of the unequal distribution of talents, capacities, and so on; indeed, being an unencumbered self 'this is true of everything about me' and so I deserve nothing at all because there is nothing intrinsic to my sense of self that could be common to all. Given this: (a) why does Rawls come to argue for the difference principle? And (b) the intuitive appeal of the difference principle can only be maintained by doing away with the idea of an unencumbered self, that is, by showing that there are in fact features of our sense of self that are shared, at least within certain communities. What is shared? For Sandel it is 'our constitutive attachments . . . as members of this family or community or nation or people or bearers of that history, as citizens of this republic', and these attachments 'allow that to some I owe more than justice requires or even permits, not by reason of agreements I have made but instead in virtue of those more or less enduring attachments and commitments that, taken together, partly define the person I am'. To imagine a person without these commitments is not to distil an individual's rational features as a free agent, but it is 'to imagine a person wholly without character' (1984: 90). This is a claim that is given an alternative rendering in Taylor's critique of individualism or, as he calls it, atomism.

Taylor (1985) argues that for liberal individualists like Rawls and Nozick society is simply an aggregate of rationally self-interested atoms: self-enclosed individuals bound to each other only through their desire to maximize their own ends in life. This view of society has important consequences for how liberal individualists view political obligation. On the atomistic account, individuals agree, through a legally binding contract, to cooperate with one another just so as to find mutual advantage in the pursuit of their individual ends. The obligation individuals feel toward each other is always mediated through this fundamental desire to further one's own ends. The liberal individualist, the atomist, therefore sees no intrinsic value in society itself (maybe even to the point of denying that society even 'exists'). So every community, including the political community itself (the state), is deemed to provide associations that are of merely instrumental rather than intrinsic value: instrumental to the pursuit of individuals' own ends rather than goods in themselves. This concept is often couched in terms of rights: the rights of the individual must take priority over the pursuit of any 'social' or 'common' good because the rights of individuals are deemed unconditional and inviolable such that they have theoretical primacy over any rights we may have as members of a group. Indeed, our obligation to society is viewed as a derivative of our individual rights and, thereby, conditional upon our consent. This consent is itself conditional upon the fact that the obligation to society must be to our rational advantage as individuals. The conclusion is that it must, therefore, be an obligation that we may choose not to give.

In contrast to the atomistic account of the relationship between individuals and social obligations, Taylor argues that we cannot ascribe natural rights without affirming the worth of certain human capacities, such as the capacity to make autonomous choices in life. Affirming these capacities, however, means that we should foster and nurture them in ourselves and in others. But certain capacities, such as our capacity to make choices for ourselves as individuals, can only develop in a society of a certain kind: that is, one that places a high value on autonomy. This is Taylor's 'social thesis': we can only become autonomous agents if we are situated in a social context where autonomy is valued, in other words a modern democratic context.

But this means that if we value individual rights then we already have an obligation to contribute to the sustenance of this kind of society. He concludes that if the social thesis is true then the 'primacy of rights' associated with atomism is impossible:

> . . . for to assert the rights in question is to affirm the capacities, and, granted the social thesis is true concerning these capacities, this commits us to an obligation to belong. This will be as fundamental as the assertion of rights, because it will be inseparable from it. So it would be incoherent to try to assert the rights, while denying the obligation or giving it the status of optional extra which we may or may not contract; this assertion is what the primacy doctrine makes. (1985: 197–8)

Against atomistic accounts, Sandel and Taylor advocate communitarianism. Communitarianism, in most of its variants (though Alasdair MacIntyre is a notable exception here), can be said to be a kind of liberal *holism* by contrast with liberal individualism. On the basis of Sandel's understanding of our 'constitutive attachments' and Taylor's social thesis, it would seem that we cannot defend individual rights without also affirming a commitment to contribute to the advancement of the kind of shared culture in which the value of autonomy is rooted – modern democratic culture. To develop our autonomy is to develop our sense of ourselves as autonomous beings, but this is not something that we can do on our own. Rather, it can only be done in dialogue with others, excavating our sense of self from within a tradition. This will provide a more secure, because less incoherent, foundation on which to secure the values of liberalism. Communitarians argue that liberalism requires an ontological theory regarding what it is to be human in a way that is not atomistic. This ontology will reveal our dependence on shared social goods and communal bonds; that is, it will be based upon 'holist' rather than 'atomist' assumptions. What does this entail? The liberal individualist stress on liberty as 'non-interference' (negative liberty) can be seen as limited in value, since real freedom involves 'self-mastery' to the extent of having the capacity developed within us to discriminate between important and less important social goods, so that we are able to pursue goods of real value – for example, distinguishing between our desires for both community and Coca-cola and recognizing that the former is of qualitatively higher value than the latter!

The development of our autonomy requires, in short, a commitment to our democratic culture that atomism itself cannot justify. This sense of commitment is usefully summed up in the notion of 'civic republicanism'. Civic republicanism begins by recognizing that individual freedom can only flourish if the social bonds that make autonomous living possible can also flourish. This means that the state in a democratic culture should aim to give expression to a shared conception of the good, while allowing individuals to exercise their capacity for choice. Furthermore, the state should encourage good citizenship in future generations by developing mechanisms for deliberation (for example, people's juries), enhancing education so that individuals are able to deliberate more effectively, and engendering a vibrant civil society full of opportunities for the kind of communal activities that unlock the shared values that are said to secure our social bonds. While the liberal atomist argues that the state must be neutral towards conceptions of the good, given reasonable pluralism, the communitarian argues that this is a chimerical notion, impossible to sustain, and therefore we must recognize that the state should be articulating a common purpose; at which point the spectre of equality rears its head again, because it is not always clear that articulating a common purpose, even one that claims to be open and responsive to diversity, will truly encompass the complex needs of all citizens – especially those who feel themselves to be on the margins of the political consensus. Will the answer to this conundrum be found in theories of democracy?

CHAPTER 5

DEMOCRACY AND POLITICAL ORDER

It is only relatively recently that democracy has become a form of government deemed by many to be beyond question: by the end of this chapter we will see that this may well be a problem for democracy itself. Until the twentieth century, democracy was often viewed with suspicion. It was thought to be a base or corrupt form of government that did not adequately take account of the (to some) obvious fact that the masses were incapable of governing themselves. For centuries, it was taken for granted that only the wise and the wealthy (and these were thought to be the same people) were deserving of a say in how society should be run. Aside from the development of liberty and equality as political ideals, two momentous events in the twentieth century apparently changed that view forever. In the aftermath of World War Two, it was no longer acceptable to assume that a charismatic individual could lead a country, because such leadership would be forever tainted with the ideological horrors of fascism. Government had to be 'by the people', not just 'of the people', if it was to avoid becoming a twisted vision of what was best 'for the people'. Moreover, the Cold War that rose from the ashes of World War Two pitted newly confident bourgeois liberal democratic views against an alternative 'communist' model of government, one that claimed to be a 'workers' democracy' but which in truth was a one-party state with few, if any, democratic credentials. Nonetheless, when market-led liberal democracies were seen to emerge victorious in 1989, with the tearing down of the Berlin Wall, the final triumph of 'rule by the people' seemed to have emerged from a battlefield many centuries old. Francis Fukuyama (1992) famously captured this sense of triumphalism as he declared the end of ideological dispute and the world-historical victory of liberal democracy in his book *The End of History and the Last Man*.

For a brief moment it seemed that the inevitable victory of democracy above other forms of government – seen as inevitable on the basis of the pseudo-Hegelianism which drove Fukuyama's analysis – was embodied within (typically) Western liberal democracies. At the end of a century of terrible conflict, it was argued, humanity had reached its final political destination: democracy.

Yet liberal democracies in the late twentieth and early twenty-first centuries have rarely looked so fragile. The internal turmoil of multicultural politics (e.g. the protests that followed the publication of Salman Rushdie's *Satanic Verses* in 1998, the furore that followed the publication of cartoons depicting Mohammed in the Danish newspaper *Jyllands-Posten*, and the race-related rioting in the suburbs of Paris, both in autumn 2005); growing dissent about political corruption; voter apathy reaching new highs; global forces that make domestic political endeavours look pointless; major economic divisions within liberal democratic societies; alienated minorities; increasingly ineffective local politics; and much more – all these developments add up to a significant 'democratic deficit' in contemporary liberal democratic politics. Moreover, the perceived illiberal and arguably undemocratic strategies and interventions that democratic countries have employed on the international stage – most notably the waging of war seen by many as illegitimate – and the difficulties associated with any kind of global democratic governance emerging from within the fractious chambers of the United Nations, suggest that the great victories of democratic thinkers, politicians and activists may be perilously close to unravelling.

In addition to these concerns, and in contrast to Fukuyama's optimism, it may well be that liberal democracy in its Western form is not the only way of achieving viable and sustainable political order. The transformation of China may be described as a process of democratization but it may produce a distinctly Chinese version of democracy, embodying Asian rather than Western values. Equally, it may be that newly resurgent Islamic countries are carving a path towards twenty-first century political order on the basis of their own values and political practices without recourse to individualist ideologies of rights and freedoms. Rather than dive into the murky sea of futurology, however, this chapter will review some of the debates at the heart of democratic theory, keeping an eye especially on whether democracy is the form of political organization that best ensures an orderly polity. The place to start is Plato's arguments against democracy, arguments that centre on the claim that democratic polities are not the best form of the republic precisely because they have a tendency to dissolve into disorder and chaos.

DEMOCRACY AND DISORDER

Plato's critique of democracy rests on three core arguments. First, he argues that the majority of people are poor judges of what is the best course for the ship of state (1974: 280–92). Most individuals, he says, judge on the basis of impulse, pity, personal bias, and so on. Even if they are trying to do the right thing, people have a tendency to let their emotions run away with them, thereby favouring some people over others. Recalling Plato's analogy of the cave (see Chapter 4), people's unreliable judgements are not surprising because the vast majority can be seen as stuck in a shadowy world of appearances, unable to contemplate the reality of things, so that in making choices they have recourse to their most immediate affections and most personal bonds with others. In contrast, as we saw, those who know the reality of things and are able to separate knowledge from opinion (the philosophers), can rule with the good of all in mind – because, in fact, they have 'seen' the good for themselves.

Secondly, Plato argues that democracy produces bad leaders. The system encourages populist sloganeering and poor decision-making in leaders because they are always tempted to enact legislation designed simply to keep the people happy. In a wonderfully evocative image, Plato compares ruling a democracy with trying to control a large unruly animal by simply 'calling what pleased it good, what annoyed it bad' (1974: 288). Democratic leaders, precisely because they must rely on the popular will of the people, are driven to regard the will of the majority as legitimate simply because it is the majority will, regardless of whether it is likely to bring the populace as a whole closer to the good life. The fear of the unruly mob overrides the claims of reason, and decision-making is robbed of the wisdom necessary to good government.

Moreover, argues Plato, democracy may maximize the liberty of its subjects, but in doing so it actually increases the tendency to factionalism, sectarianism and tribalism within the polity. The people may want to be free, but do they really want the disagreement and conflict that often follows the free expression of political ideas? According to Plato, the people would rather be secure in their place as part of a smooth-running polity than to have their freedom at the risk of their security. In case this sounds rather patronizing, it is worth considering whether Plato was right in this regard given recent security legislation in the wake of the 'war on terror' (for example, legislation that allows for longer detention of 'terror suspects' and increased use of surveillance techniques). Democracy and freedom are intimately connected, as Plato realized, but freedom alone does not justify democracy: freedom is a value that we (should?) all too willingly sacrifice for the sake of (non-democratic) political order. But, Plato continues, democratic freedoms not only lead to tribalism: they also increase the tendency towards permissiveness; free expression, he recognized, often takes the form of licentiousness, be it in the form of sex, drugs or poetry (Plato's rock-and-roll)! For Plato such freedom is illusory, stuck as it is in the rut of pursuing immediate pleasures. More fundamentally, though, such uses of freedom simply increase the social fragmentation caused by democratic tribalism.

But what is wrong with such free expression? And we moderns see diversity, not fragmentation. But Plato argues that democracy is simply unsustainable. The conflicts it contains mean that it will never be the root of a stable political order. In fact, Plato argues that the chief danger of democracy is that it will lead to a social and political dissolution where order can only be restored through tyranny. It is not a benevolent tyranny of the wise that will be required, but the more straightforward tyranny of the despotic. In the end, it is this that condemns democracy as a form of government, according to Plato: democracy cannot be the best form of government because it will inevitably lead to tyranny.

DEMOCRACY AND THE VALUE OF POLITICAL PARTICIPATION

Two millennia later, J. S. Mill turned these arguments around, so to speak, in a famous defence of representative government. He defended democracy precisely on the grounds that to participate in government was to maximize one's intellectual and moral capacities and thereby achieve a sense of pleasure that is qualitatively higher than the merely transitory base pleasures of life. The discussion appears in Mill's *Considerations on Representative Government*, published in 1861, at a time when the value of representative government could not be taken for granted. There was a lurking Platonism in middle-class Victorian ideas about politics: if only the wise were allowed to get on with ruling, it was often thought, the rest of well-to-do Victorian society could get on with whatever other pursuits kept Victorian ladies and gentlemen entertained. Mill thought it wise to address this issue directly, and he constructed a simple thought-experiment to expose the issues at stake. His thought-experiment envisages a benevolent despot, and begins with the following question: would being ruled by a benevolent despot be better than having to take part in political life ourselves?

The benevolent despot Mill has in mind does not have any of the human vices that would make us dislike his despotic rule. The true, if imaginary, benevolent despot is wise, thoughtful, equipped with all the information necessary for good decisions, and certainly not prone to corruption or thirsty for power. So, the all too obvious impracticality of a genuinely benevolent despot is put to one side by Mill so that he can get to the heart of the matter: if the benevolent despot really was making the best political decisions for us, would this be the best form of government? It is fair to say that we can see the attraction. We might imagine more time to do the things we want – carpentry, dancing and metaphysics, for example – without the burdens of having to engage with pesky politicians on our doorstep and those boring programmes about politics on TV. Indeed, the attraction of not having to participate in politics is part of the package of ideas that motivate liberal demands to 'roll back the state'. There are many individuals who would welcome a life without politics if they could guarantee the benevolence of Mill's despot: they would welcome such a system because they could enjoy their freedoms without the burden of political involvement to secure those freedoms. Perhaps many individuals in contemporary liberal democracies are a bit more Victorian than we often think!

J. S. Mill argued, however, that to forgo political participation, even if a truly benevolent despot were to dominate the political scene, would be a disaster for our sense of ourselves as rational, moral and religious beings. With regard to our intellectual capabilities, Mill argues that life under a benevolent despot would lead to the stunting of our capacities for rational inquiry and progressive thought. He argues that generating knowledge always needs an outlet, and that we must be able to apply our findings in order for them to be tested, acknowledged and improved. Under a benevolent despot, however, the very possibility of such applied knowledge would be entirely at the whim of the despot, and we would quickly lose the desire to even strive for intellectual progress in the face of such arbitrariness. With regard to our moral sensibility, the argument is similar. Mill remarks that 'the food of feeling is action' (1972: 220), by which he means that without an outlet to pursue new ways of life, not just argue about moral theory, individuals will become deadened to those around them, and humanity as a whole will suffer because people will learn to feel nothing. One might think that despite all this one could find solace in the religious domain. But Mill sees no such option, as any religion that is allowed to remain under the benevolent despot would be devoid of a social role, and become 'the most selfish and contracted egoism'. In sum, no matter how wise and benevolent the despot, without the means to develop our intellectual, moral and religious capacities to the full, which must include developing them within the public domain, we would become stunted creatures unable to think rationally, morally or religiously. This would be a disaster because the aim of all good government, Mill assumes, is the improvement of the people.

If benevolent despotism does not improve the people, which form of government would? For Mill, the benevolent despot thought-experiment makes it clear: 'the ideally best form of government is that in which every citizen not only has a voice in the exercise of sovereignty but who also takes part in some public function' (1972: 223). It is notable that Mill does not think of 'the ideally best form of government' as one in which everyone has a say: rather, it is one in which everyone participates 'in some public function'. This concept of commitment to public duty gives rise to many interesting features of Mill's defence of representative democracy, and of particular note is his defence of 'public voting'. He argues that it is the duty of each elector to put their own selfish interests to one side and to 'consider the interest of the public' (1972: 326). Voting in private, out of sight in a polling booth, does not encourage this, so Mill argues that we should all vote in a public forum: our preferences should be known so that we are forced to justify the extent to which we have based our vote on public, not private, interests. It does, at least, mean that we can all perform 'some public function' simply by voting, although Mill hoped for a deeper engagement with political life than by this alone.

But what are the benefits of active political participation? What improvements would it bring to the people? Whatever trials are involved in political life, Mill believed that public life brought with it the kind of long-term benefits that a life without it would surely make impossible. He claims, for example: 'the maximum of the invigorating effect of freedom upon the character is only obtained when the person acted on either is, or is looking forward to becoming, a citizen as fully privileged as any other' (1972: 232). While we may feel a momentary burst of freedom as we give ourselves up to the benevolent despot, this feeling will only diminish and wither as we realize that we are deprived of control over our own intellectual, moral and spiritual lives. For all the hard work of being in politics, the benefit to individuals of political participation is that each will feel an ever greater sense of freedom as he/she becomes more involved and more able to take control over their lives. The benefit to society is that free individuals will pursue intellectual, moral and spiritual projects that will lead to the progress of all in society.

But, as it stands, this is an argument for political participation; it is not in itself an argument for representative government. Mill must consider the following question: what kind of government will maximize participation, and thereby instil in people the maximum invigorating effect of freedom? It is interesting that Mill considers *communism* may be the form of government that promotes the kind of political participation which will benefit society. However, he ultimately dismisses this possibility. He concedes that a communist form of organization may be appropriate for a small, highly educated elite of Victorian society (Mill was a great defender of 'experiments in living'), but given the impossibility of the great mass of people living up to the ideals of communism (individuals are too selfish, he presumes), and given that only small-scale communities could even get close to the ideal, he argues that the best form of government, the one that maximizes 'the invigorating effect of freedom', must be representative government.

This defence of representative government rests on a distinction made famous by Mill in his critique and revision of Jeremy Bentham's version of utilitarianism. Whereas Bentham argued that 'push pin is as good as poetry', that all sources of happiness are equivalent, Mill argued that there are some pleasures that are qualitatively higher than other pleasures. In order to make his point he claimed that it is 'better to be a human being dissatisfied than a pig satisfied, better to be Socrates dissatisfied than a fool satisfied' (1972: 10). In other words, no matter how unhappy one might be as a human, one will always be capable of experiencing pleasures that are immeasurably higher than those that the pig feels rolling around in the mud. More controversially perhaps, he continues by saying that no matter how miserable a life of questioning and doubt makes a philosopher like Socrates, he will always be happier than the contented fool who seeks his or her short-term pleasures from the latest soap-opera or video game (or the Platonic equivalent). Whether or not one agrees with this, there is good reason to think that political participation, as Mill argues, is one way of achieving a sense of higher pleasure. The more one participates in the life of the *polis*, the freer one becomes and the closer one is to tasting higher pleasures. Political participation is a key component of the 'energetic' life that Mill advocated (even though it was a very intellectual sense of the energetic life that he had in mind). The energetic political participation that good representative government requires, according to Mill, becomes the source of the free and open discussion that he believes is a prerequisite for the progress of humanity, towards ever more fulfilling forms of existence.

As invigorating as this argument is, it raises some important questions that must be noted before moving on. Should government be about improving people? It may be that government should do more than provide a basic security structure (akin to Hobbes' *Leviathan*), and that beyond this it is up to individuals themselves to decide whether or not to improve themselves – and, if they choose to do so, whether they play push-pin or read philosophy. Is Mill asking too much of us in terms of political participation? He is a paradigmatic example of a general tendency in political philosophy: the tendency to assume that everyone should be a political philosopher. It is a presumption that underpins many an inspiring vision, but is it realistic and, more importantly, is it even desirable? Is participation in politics necessary to maintain one's freedom? Mill's vision of the freedom that results from an active engagement in political life is actually in tension with his defence of liberty as a space of non-interference. While these two ideas can, in principle, be reconciled, questions must be asked about where the lines are to be drawn between Mill's commitment to privacy and his advocacy of public service. Most fundamentally of all, though, can we distinguish between higher and lower pleasures? Is it not simply middle-class Victorian elitism to suggest that reading poetry is a source of higher pleasure than playing parlour games? Perhaps Mill is confusing his personal preference for poetry with a preference that everyone would share? Indeed, if pleasure is a matter of subjective choice then there would be no grounds for assuming that there are higher or lower pleasures. If one pursues this line then it is hard to see how Mill could justify political participation in the way that he does. However, many other political philosophers have taken different routes to justifying democratic government, and we can get a flavour of these through a brief history of the difficult birth of liberal democracies.

THE DIFFICULT BIRTH OF LIBERAL DEMOCRACY

Modernity began to dawn throughout Europe from the sixteenth century onwards, characterized by social, economic and intellectual changes including exponential increases in industrialization, a wide range of scientific and technological advances that transformed production and communication, and, crucially, a newly dominant bourgeois class of entrepreneurs looking to exploit these changes for profit. Medieval Europe had embedded hierarchical polities based on the supposed divine right of kings, but challenges to this feudal order came rapidly as economies and societies modernized. An era of rebellion and revolution was established as the new bourgeoisie fought to gain control over the political structures that were hindering their industrial advances. Democracy was born as the political form of a process of modernization, its roots deep in the social and economic transformation of production. It is this process that explains why 'democracy' and 'capitalism' appear to us today as intimately interwoven. From a normative perspective, the concepts that link these terms are liberty and equality, because democracy is often viewed as the political expression of the individual liberty and equality which are essential for the smooth running of the free market.

Thinking about liberty first, the ideal of democracy was set against the feudal forms of paternalistic governance with a view to ensuring the freedom of individuals. But within this broad conception, two distinct ideas can be discerned. The first is that democratic government will protect the interests of the people by endowing them with rights that act as claims against an overbearing state. Such claims would challenge the legitimacy of state authorities, and oppose unwarranted intrusion in one's private life. This is what we might call a *classical liberal* view of democracy. The second conception of democracy that emerged from the ashes of feudalism was founded on the idea that the value of democracy is embodied by the idea of a 'free state'. On this account, personal liberty and the liberty of the state are intimately and irremovably bound together. There is, therefore, a duty incumbent on a democratic state to protect all its members by encouraging them to be good citizens. This is the *civic republican* view of democracy. Locke is a good example of the classical liberal democrat, Rousseau of the civic republican variety, and Mill has elements of both.

Although these two visions of the democratic polity overlap, they offer distinct ideas of the value of democracy. Moreover, they are rather messily entwined in the birth of actual democratic governments, and their contrasting demands have raised questions which persist in contemporary liberal democratic societies. For example, is it the function of democratic government to protect private interests, or to foster public duty? Who are 'the people' of a democratic state: a group of isolated individuals, or a community bound together by shared interests? Should the good citizen be thought of as one who gets on with his/her life simply without breaking any laws, or someone who helps to maintain the democratic *polis* itself? These questions are all examples of how the liberal and republican visions of democratic life continue to conflict with each other. Fundamentally they arise because democrats are often confused about whether it is individual freedom or collective freedom that they are defending. One way forward is to consider that other great democratic value: equality.

Democratic government is not simply about the protection of liberty or the promotion of a free state: it is also fundamentally about the equality of each person in the state to have a say in government. 'One person, one vote' encapsulates this central egalitarian dimension of the democratic ideal. The animating idea here is that the only way to demonstrate that everybody is equal is by everybody having an equal say in the running of government. This egalitarian dimension to democracy denies any natural inequalities between individuals (such as those defended by advocates of the divine rights of kings). Whether the freedom that comes with democracy is individual and/or collective, perhaps the most important aspect of democratic government is that it treats us all as equally worthy of respect, whether artisan or aristocrat.

And yet, this egalitarian dimension of the democratic ideal is not as clear-cut as it may appear. We shall see in the next section how the representative nature of liberal democracies can work against the ideal of equal influence in government. But it is worth noting that democratic equality has often been thought to conflict with the pursuit of democratic liberty. In the nineteenth century Alexis de Tocqueville argued, in his influential book *Democracy in America*, that the increasing drive towards equality in US democracy was a threat to individual liberty because it led to the 'tyranny of the majority'. As noted in Chapter 2, this was a view that greatly inspired J. S. Mill, who gave the idea prominence by arguing that such tyranny emerges when 'the people . . . may desire to oppress a part of their number'; and, he continued, it is 'now generally regarded as one of the evils against which society requires to be on its guard' (1972: 73). Mill also recognized the 'tyranny of the majority' as the tendency of majorities towards mediocrity, poor governance, and the pursuit of short-term satisfaction. The attendant danger, he thought, was the stifling of social and political experimentation, long-term planning, and wise decision-making which are essential for the liberty of individuals and peoples.

FROM REPRESENTATIVE TO DELIBERATIVE DEMOCRACY

Liberal democracies were born with conflicting ideals at their heart, and they have had to wage a constant battle of ideas against elitist detractors – even to the point of trying to incorporate such criticisms *a là* Mill – and, as a consequence, democracy today faces numerous internal and external challengers who are possibly growing in confidence. The general plight of contemporary liberal democracies has been and continues to be a source of concern for democratic theorists in political philosophy. How are these problems to be overcome? There is general agreement that, as Al Smith (an unsuccessful Democratic candidate for the US Presidency in 1928) said: 'the only cure for the evils of democracy is more democracy'. But what would 'more democracy' involve?

Let us first try to clarify some problems of representative democracy, beyond the difficulty democrats have in trying to be both libertarians and egalitarians. At stake is the very idea of representation itself. Generally speaking we can split the question of representation into two: 'who is being represented?' and 'is representation desirable or even possible?' With regard to the former, it is common in liberal democracies to find oneself in the minority from time to time. This is usually not too problematic because one will be in the majority on other occasions. But what if one finds oneself in a (relatively) permanent minority? If, in this instance, one has no effective influence on the running of government, it is fair to say that democracy enhances neither one's freedom nor one's equality. Representatives are supposed to represent the whole of society but it seems unlikely that this could ever be the case, especially as the global movement of peoples makes nation-states more internally heterogeneous. We should therefore consider whether our politicians should be seen as representatives at all. Edmund Burke addressed this concern in his acceptance speech on becoming a Member of Parliament in 1774. Acknowledging that an MP should 'ever, and in all cases' prioritize the interests of his constituents above his own, Burke nonetheless declared to the audience that '[an MP's] unbiased opinion, his enlightened conscience, his mature judgement, he ought not to sacrifice to you; to any man, or to any set of men living' (1996: 68–9). For Burke, it was the duty of the elected member to engage with the complex apparatus of government as one *delegated* to do so with wisdom and courage, and not as one who merely seeks to represent the interests of his constituents. Burke accepted this as a responsibility bestowed on him by being elected. For Benjamin Barber, a contemporary political philosopher, the lack of representation in representative democracy is a failing that penetrates to its core: 'the representative principle steals from individuals the ultimate responsibility for their values, beliefs, and actions' (1984: 145).

At the root of such claims is the argument that it is theoretically impossible to give full and adequate representation to anything, let alone a 'thing' as complex as multifaceted as a constituency. Iris Marion Young, for example, has used Jacques Derrida's famous deconstruction of the philosophy of presence to unravel the complex assumptions we make when we seek to justify the representative nature of liberal democracies. She argues:

> If we accept the argument that representation is necessary, but we also accept an image of democratic decision-making as requiring a co-presence of citizens, and that representation is legitimate only if in some way the representative is identical with the constituency, then we have a paradox: representation is necessary but impossible. (2000: 126)

Young argues that there is a way out of this paradox, if we reconceptualize representation so that it no longer implies substituting one identity for another (the identity of the representative for that of the constituents), but implies instead a 'processual' relation between constituents and their representative. Such a relation would be premised on the difference and separation between the two, rather than on their identity. In truth, this is an alternative route to Burke's point that the representative must connect with the constituents, but should never confuse this with having to speak as if she or he were the voice of the constituents.

For all that the idea of delegation rather than representation must be recognized, it tends to shore up rather than alleviate a pressing problem for modern democratic regimes. In short, the idea of the delegate means that the electorate tend to drift away from politics except when they have to vote for their next delegate, by which time they have often lost interest anyway, so they may not even care who is delegated to speak on behalf of their constituency. There may be a tendency for representative systems to increase the distance between the people and the world of politics, and much empirical evidence seems to confirm this. Many problems could result from this, and if we recall Mill's defence of representative democracy we may agree with Barber that 'under a representative government the voter is free only on the day he casts his ballot' (1984: 145). This describes a difficulty that has led many defenders of democracy to construct alternatives visions of a democratic system, the most popular being *deliberative democracy*.

Deliberative democracy is a model of democratic government that seems to overcome the failings of the purely representative model by placing a large emphasis on the value of 'deliberation'. Deliberation, in this context, refers to a process, or more often processes, of rational argumentation. The central claim, therefore, is that voting is not enough to sustain democracy. Rather, democracy will only be sustained by people participating in debate and discussion, intending to reach a reasonable consensus on the contested political issues. One of the insights that underpin deliberative theory is that debate and discussion, if rationally undertaken, can lead us to transform our opinions and preferences. So democracy on this basis is not simply about aggregating individual preferences and pleasing the majority – with the attendant dangers of the 'tyranny of the majority' that this creates: it is, instead, a process whereby people will in most cases move beyond their first opinions because they will have reasonably considered the opinions of others involved in the decision-making procedure. James Bohman sums up the ideal of deliberative democracy well, as 'a dialogical process of exchanging reasons for the purpose of resolving problematic situations that cannot be settled without interpersonal co-ordination and co-operation' (1996: 27). Put like this, however, the ideal of deliberative democracy may sound too idealistic to ever come to fruition. But it is worth examining the theoretical framework that most deliberative theorists appeal to, as developed by Jürgen Habermas, whose theories of communicative action and discourse ethics provide the core normative basis for the deliberative model of democracy.

Habermas's (1984, 1987, 1990) work can be described as the attempt to rescue the Enlightenment democratic vision in the wake of its rather one-sided and distorted incorporation into modern Western democratic culture. The fundamental problem with the classic Enlightenment project was that it assumed that every individual was a rational being, and that this alone was sufficient to ensure a rational society once everybody had realized their own rationality. Habermas argued instead that we cannot presume that our own idea of a rational solution to a problem is one that all other rational beings will share. Rather, we have to present our reasons through argumentation and debate, and only when we have reached a consensus can we say that we have found the properly rational course of action. The innovative aspect of Habermas's claims in this regard, however, is that he turns to everyday language use to construct this properly dialogical conception of human rationality. If we understand the presuppositions of human communication, argues Habermas, then we will be able to understand the democratic potential of debate and discussion.

Habermas describes conversation where everyone involved is concerned to reach an understanding with one another as 'communicative action'. According to him, when we use language communicatively we make certain presuppositions: most importantly, that if we genuinely want to reach an understanding then we must presuppose that we will each be motivated by force of reason alone – not by the desire to 'win the argument', or 'control the others involved'; not motivated, that is, by the desire for power, violence, profit or coercion. A non-genuine agreement is merely a *de facto accord*, when we agree because of the power imbalance involved; that would be a coerced agreement as a result of the strategic action of one of the participants. As Habermas expresses it, if we are genuinely looking to reach an understanding with others through communication then we will be motivated solely by the 'unforced force of the better argument'. Communicative action, therefore, is premised on a non-instrumental use of reason: reason is not treated as a means to any other end, but as a good in itself. A communicatively reached agreement is not about one person treating another as an object; in philosophical terms it is not based on a subject-object relationship, but rather on a genuinely *intersubjective* relationship: a relationship between people. The founders of the Enlightenment did not give sufficient consideration to this important aspect of reasoning because they assumed that all reasonable people would simply reach the same rational conclusion without the need for dialogue. Habermas acknowledges that few, if any, real dialogues are devoid of the distorting influence of money or power, and driven only by a desire for the better argument. Nonetheless, he argues that the intuitive plausibility of the distinction between a reasonable and a forced agreement means that we presuppose in our everyday conversations the possibility of what he calls 'an ideal speech situation'.

The claim that language use contains the outlines of an ideal speech situation gives defenders of deliberative democracy hope that rational discussion will give substance to the democratic ideal that mere representation lacks. But are we not back to a very idealistic set of claims? How does Habermas justify his view that everyday language implies an ideal speech situation? While there are many long answers to this question, for our purposes we can distil one short answer, and consider three that emerge from it. The main claim is that language use oriented towards rational understanding must be given a theoretical priority over language use oriented towards a strategic end. Habermas defends this principal claim in three ways. First, he argues that strategic action is parasitic upon communicative action in that one cannot use language for one's own gain if one does not already know how to use language to try to reach an understanding with another person. Secondly, he claims that language learning is inherently communicative in that we would never learn our native language, or any other, were it not possible to reach a set of understandings with other speakers. Thirdly, and most importantly, he argues that communicative action is the source of the 'reproduction of the lifeworld'. The term 'lifeworld' is one Habermas takes from the philosopher Edmund Husserl, and it refers to the background horizon of meanings that foster cultural reproduction, social integration and socialization. Habermas argues that if we only ever acted strategically it would not be possible to sustain this background horizon of meanings, since to act purely for oneself is to break the bonds of sociality. Indeed, to act strategically all the time would be to abstract oneself from the social world altogether – and, in his view, schizophrenia or suicide would result.

Whether or not one accepts these arguments in support of the claim that an ideal speech situation is deeply embedded in every act of communication, it is crucial to Habermas's claims that we can distinguish between a legitimate agreement based on rational discussion and an illegitimate one that has been forged in the fires of money and power. With regard to politics, the key issue is whether or not we can reach this genuine agreement about the norms governing our interaction. In Habermas's schema, when we look to address the issue of norms we are using communication for an ethical purpose, and he describes this process as 'discourse ethics'. According to Habermas (1990), if we are trying to reach agreement about the norms which should govern society then a non-coerced dialogue aimed at mutual understanding will, in principle, produce a rationally justifiable outcome. In other words, a genuine discourse that does not have the distortions of power and money at play within it will give rise to norms of social cooperation which all can consent to, irrespective of their own view of the good. If this is the case then we can certainly see the attraction for democratic theorists. Discourse ethics is based on the idea that we can reach rational agreement about how best to get on with each other in the long term – not just making temporary political pacts that may dissolve at the next election, but rather accepting the force of the better argument. If democracy is a way of ensuring that all have a say in government then it should be better to encourage everyone to reach a permanent rational consensus, rather than simply let them voice their opinion periodically, for example every five years or so at a general election.

Is deliberative democracy practicable? How can one achieve the goal of rationally motivated consensus in complex modern societies? Much of the current literature on deliberative democracy is focused on these and related questions because the criticisms that have been levelled at this as a model of democracy have tended to dwell on the utopian nature of the deliberative ideal. Bohman sums up the problem facing those who wish to institutionalize deliberation when he says 'either decision-making institutions gain effectiveness at the cost of democratic deliberation or they retain democracy at the cost of effective decision-making' (1998: 422). But according to Bohman this is a dilemma that can be overcome, and he along with other theorists of deliberative democracy has used this dilemma as a springboard for some very inventive applied political philosophy. While it is not possible to summarize all the interesting initiatives that have been proposed, we can broadly divide them into those that aim to reinvigorate the existing democratic structures, and those that suggest new procedures to augment our existing democracies. Crucial to both is the aim of creating a lively citizenry looking to actively engage in a civil society richly populated with opportunities for collective debate and discussion.

In terms of reinvigorating existing political structures, the first port of call is usually political parties. Political parties have tended to become bureaucratic machines oriented towards success at the polls. If they could be rejuvenated through the principles of deliberative democracy, they could become sites for genuine debate and discussion to enable the presentation of policies based on what is best for society, rather than policies oriented simply towards winning the vote. For all that this sounds very far away from the reality of current political parties it is by no means beyond the realms of possibility that they could become the embodiment, in part at least, of the deliberative ideal. Thinking about relatively new ways of institutionalizing deliberation, a lot of emphasis has been placed upon citizen juries. These are collections of individuals (usually chosen by lot, like a jury, from the whole electorate) tasked with debating key policy issues. The aim is to create a microcosm of deliberation that can be used to infer what the broader population would conclude were they all to engage in such a debate. There are undoubtedly problems with this idea, but there has also been some empirical work done on these juries which suggests that the deliberative hope of transforming initially selfish opinions into more reasonable consensus driven conclusions is manifest in these small-scale experiments. The task for advocates of deliberation is to envisage ways in which these small successes can be expanded into the kind of decision-making processes that would be necessary in complex modern societies.

But it is not just the practical problems that deliberative democratic theorists face. The fundamental issue is whether or not deliberation will lead to better decisions: that is, decisions that are qualitatively more rational than those reached by a simple aggregation of opinions. Does deliberation really transform an opinionated view into a rational one?

Is consensus possible, even in theory? Besides, we may value democracy precisely because it allows diversity and dissensus to flourish, and we may want to question an ideal of democracy that places such a strong emphasis on agreement. These are some of the questions and issues raised by critics of deliberative democracy who, nonetheless, wish to defend a 'radical' ideal of democracy as the means by which we can keep disagreement and dissent alive within the political world.

AGONISM AND POLITICAL ORDER

The emergence of radical democracy, as an identifiable strand of democratic theorizing, is usually associated with the publication of Ernesto Laclau's and Chantal Mouffe's (1985) *Hegemony and Socialist Strategy: Towards a Radical Democratic Politics.* Employing a mixture of Marxism and poststructuralism (Chapter 3), they have developed a critique of those contemporary theories that fail to recognize the 'social antagonisms' that actually structure the political world we inhabit. Whereas philosophers of democracy tend to emphasize community, agreement, consensus and rationality, Laclau and Mouffe argue that these ideas misconstrue the basic disagreements that give rise to politics in the first place. Only a radical conception of democracy, they argue, could enable these differences to co-exist. In relation to Habermas and other deliberative theorists, for example, Laclau and Mouffe stress that they share the desire to transcend the limitations of a representative, aggregative and majoritarian model, but they also argue that the basic nature of social antagonism means that they cannot conceive of the possibility of 'any kind of rational consensus'. 'For us,' they say, 'a non-exclusive public sphere of rational argument is a conceptual impossibility' (1985: xvii). It is paradoxical, they argue, to use the ideal of consensus to regulate democratic processes, because democracy is premised upon disagreement: dissensus is necessary, they say, for the functioning of democracy, and any attempt to remove it (even in theory) is actually striking at the heart of the democratic project itself. As Laclau and Mouffe put it: 'we maintain that without conflict and division, a pluralist democratic politics would be impossible' (1985: xvii).

This concern with the deliberative desire for consensus, as we can see, is based on a very different conception of the democratic community. As Jacques Ranciere (1995, 1999) has argued, the paradox of democracy is that every democracy must claim to include everyone, but must actually exclude some of the people it is supposed to represent. The presumption behind such claims is that 'the people' of Lincoln's 'of the people, by the people, for the people' simply do not exist as a pre-political entity; either as a mass of individuals with interests that can be managed, or as a community of shared values. Rather, 'the people' are the product of political processes, but 'the people' never includes everyone. Are 'the people' those who inhabit a certain territory, those who have a shared vision, those who are born or live in a particular country, and so on? Given these problems, it is argued, the ideal of democratic community is as illusory as that of democratic consensus.

Indeed, as Laclau, Mouffe and Ranciere would all agree, terms like 'liberal democracy' do not designate particular forms of political organization – rather, they are hegemonic terms that certain states claim in order to secure legitimacy in the population that is being governed. It is this set of claims that has led Adrian Little (2008) to argue that the ideal of 'democracy' has become an article of faith because it seems incapable of rational justification. More worryingly, he goes on, defenders of democracy have become 'increasingly pious' in that they abhor attempts to complicate the idea of democracy by drawing out its links with violence and the contradictions of democratic institutions. Bringing these themes together, Little says: 'The failure to disrupt and evaluate the concept of democracy certainly augments its hegemonic power but, as Ranciere argues, it also weakens it because what masquerades as democratic piety today is actually a form of hatred of democracy' (2008: 165).

As this makes clear, though, for all the vehemence of the critique, the goal is still the defence of democracy. So, what alternative is offered by the radical democrats? As we noted in the case of deliberative democracy, such questions are not easy to answer: criticism tends to be easier if it doesn't have to be constructive. Nonetheless, there are some political philosophers who have grappled with the tricky issue of trying to articulate what democracy would require, to be worthy of the term 'radical'. I shall briefly mention the work of William Connolly.

For Connolly (1991, 1995), the main task of radical democratic politics is to keep diversity and pluralism alive and well in democracies. On the grounds that the political world is constituted by deep and irreducible pluralities of view, the aim is not to reconcile these differences through discussion but to create structures through which they can be recognized and respected without subjugation. For Connolly, this requires an 'ethos of pluralization': an approach to life that actively seeks to create 'new, positive identities' within the political sphere itself. Democracy, for Connolly, is not a project to be completed, but an ongoing process which facilitates the creation of new social identities while recognizing that these identities will never be able to form a cohesive single identity which democratic institutions could represent. Instead, the institutions of democracy should look to 'absorb' antagonistic relationships by fostering 'agonistic respect'. Such respect, according to Connolly, involves more than liberal toleration: it requires that we appreciate different political positions and recognize that every position, including our own, is contingent and contestable. Eschewing a firm footing for our political convictions, we will come to respect each others' differences without seeking to reconcile them through discussion.

That said, and although Connolly's vision offers a timely warning against the potential dangers of consensus, he can still not shake off the counter-claim that his theorizations are marked by an 'institutional deficit' (Howarth, 2008) – at which point the problem of political order returns. Plato argued that democracy brought dissolution and decay and that these social ills, once established, could be cured only by the painful medicine of tyranny. Radical democrats seek to celebrate and maintain the diversity of political opinions and ways of life that democracy requires. But, if we cannot detail the institutional arrangements that would enable this to happen, can we be sure that the pluralization of pluralism would not, in the end, necessitate a return to tyranny in the name of social and political order? This problem seems particularly acute when we consider the demands of multicultural societies, composed as they are of radically different cultures seeking legitimacy within one democratic state.

CHAPTER 6

CULTURE AND CRITIQUE

Many of the debates and discussions in the previous chapters have revolved around the question: who are we? Admittedly, putting it like this sounds both too simplistic and too profound, but it is nonetheless true to say that the answer one gives to this question will certainly influence the position one adopts within the conversation of political philosophy. In the normative mainstream of political philosophy, and as discussed in Chapter 4, the answers to this question tend to split in two. There are those that will claim that we are fundamentally individuals endowed with reason and capable of making autonomous choices on our own behalf; these are the *individualists*. There are others who claim that we are the products of our upbringing in the sense that our cultural heritage plays a central role in the constitution of our sense of self: these are the *communitarians*. We can see the tension between these two approaches if we explore the relationship of an individual to his or her culture by way of two of the most prominent debates in contemporary political philosophy. First, there is the debate around the phenomena of multiculturalism, especially in modern liberal democracies. Secondly, there is a closely related debate that centres on the embeddedness, or not, of our identity within cultural traditions, especially in a world where globalization has taken hold. We shall see that central to both is the need to think through the idea of critique, and we will turn to hermeneutics and critical theory toward the end of the chapter to see if these philosophical frameworks help to clarify the problems we have encountered.

BACKGROUND TO THE CULTURE DEBATES

It is important to set the scene for these debates. Anglo-American political philosophy of the last three decades has increasingly reflected one of the big challenges facing liberal democracies: how to respond to the growing number of minority cultural groups that are seeking recognition and rights in liberal states. Culture has come to replace class as the principal marker and divider of people, and political theorists have had to revise their normative principles in order to respond to this (gender, as always, remains marginal – but more on this below and in the next chapter). In many respects, the cultural groups that have found their voice are those that are the product of complex processes of immigration and assimilation (or non-assimilation), but it is equally true to say that this upsurge of interest in culture has led 'indigenous peoples' to express their concerns with ever greater confidence and clarity. Indeed, the issue of whether or not cultural groups should be given special status (and, if so, what kind of status) within the political constitutions and institutions of their respective states is one that continues to vex contemporary political philosophers. In particular, general concerns about culture have come to focus on whether or not minority cultures, or cultures under threat from the dominant culture within a territory, should be given special rights to protect the central aspects of that culture – such as rights that seek to protect their native language. As we shall see, one of the key issues underpinning this debate is whether or not 'we individuals' are defined, in some important and irremovable manner, by the cultural baggage we carry.

For individualists the correct response to the culture debate is very straightforward. Individualists are committed to the idea that every person (with a few standard exceptions relating to age, reasonableness and the like) is defined as such by being able to choose what to value in life and what goals to pursue, and by choosing to define him/herself in certain ways rather than others. On this conception of the person, choice rather than identity is emphasized, and identity is treated as fundamentally a matter of one's own choice. By extension, individualists typically assume that shared goods, values shared by a community, have only an *extrinsic* worth; by which they mean that such benefits are only valuable if they are instrumental to the individual's own ends in life. These deep foundational claims about who we are lead individualists to argue that there can be no grounds for defending the idea that cultures are social entities worthy of rights; for the individualist it doesn't make sense to say that an entire culture should be given rights, because 'a culture' is only a secondary social formation in the sense that it is no more than the contingently shared interests of the individuals that constitute it. Moreover, any attempt to defend the idea that cultures should be afforded certain rights is dangerous, from an individualist perspective; the danger being that 'cultural rights' may well conflict with the rights of individuals. In the case of such conflict, if cultural rights are deemed to triumph over basic individual rights, then the desire to protect cultures will lead to the oppression of individuals (we will say more about this below).

Individualists typically recall that the opposition to cultural rights stems from the strong egalitarian presumptions of liberalism. Most importantly, such opposition stems from the claim that all individuals should be treated with equal respect *regardless* of sex, race, ethnicity and cultural background. Most individualists, therefore, consider themselves to be expressing the basic intuition of liberalism: that the constitution, and the principal organs of the state (what Rawls would call 'the basic structure' – see Chapter 4) should reflect this egalitarian presumption by being 'difference-blind'. We can recall the Rawlsian ideas of 'the original position' and 'the veil of ignorance' as devices that give vivid expression to this egalitarian and 'difference-blind' impetus within liberalism. The alternative, many liberal individualists would argue, is to defend a 'separate but equal' policy which was the bedrock of apartheid and many other systems which infringe the rights of individuals.

Communitarian critics of individualism argue that the individualist emphasis on choice over identity is inconsistent (see Taylor's argument against atomism in Chapter 4) and, moreover, that we have good grounds to view our cultural heritage as *intrinsic* to our identity because it provides a source for our values, beliefs and goals in life. What is more, they argue that individualists do not have a monopoly on liberalism. Far from it: a more consistent and sensitive form of liberalism emerges from communitarian conceptions of who we are. As one example of this they point out that the risk of a 'separate but equal' policy that might result from assigning rights to cultures is overplayed. In particular, it misses the crucial distinction between the imposition of segregation (for example African American segregation in parts of the USA up to the 1960s) and the choice that some groups make to retain their distinctiveness from mainstream culture (for example the celebration of traditions and customs by the aboriginal peoples of Australia). In the former case groups were forcibly *excluded* from the system of government and structures of society; in the latter case, groups are resisting forcible *inclusion* or assimilation. Surely, the communitarians argue, true liberals should be able to conceive of rights for cultural groups that would enable their distinctiveness to be maintained in the face of dominant, usually white Anglo-American, cultural imposition? For liberal communitarians, liberalism should be concerned with not only the respect due to each citizen as an individual, but also the cultures that are being oppressed and in some cases under a real threat of extinction.

CULTURAL MEMBERSHIP AS A PRIMARY GOOD

Navigating the choppy seas around the cultural archipelago of liberal norms has led to many examples of innovative and challenging political philosophy. Perhaps the best known is that of Will Kymlicka (1989, 1995). Kymlicka argues that cultural membership must be valued on the basis that it is good for individuals, and that other liberals (of a more staunchly individualist outlook) have been wrong not to recognize its significance. In particular, he argues that some individuals, members of minority cultures, are disadvantaged in relation to the good of cultural membership, and that this disadvantage justifies the provision of special rights for those cultures. Kymlicka is not, however, a communitarian political philosopher. We can see how he walks this tightrope by turning to his elaboration of the idea of cultural membership as a primary good.

In *A Theory of Justice* Rawls developed the idea of 'primary goods'. He defines these as all the effective means necessary for the pursuit of a rational plan of life, such as basic liberties and equal opportunities, and also wealth, power, education and self-respect. While the individuals in the hypothetical original position do not know their conception of the good, Rawls assumes that they will prefer more rather than fewer primary goods (1972: 93). Kymlicka argues that Rawls misses out one important primary good: the good of cultural membership. Cultural membership is a primary good because having a culture enables individuals to establish meaning within their lives. In other words, cultural possession should be part of the package of primary goods that allow us to conceive of how best to live our lives, whatever it is that we value in life, and therefore it must be defended along with the basic liberties and rights expressed by Rawls's principles of justice. Individuals, in short, need a secure culture if they are to have a reasonable opportunity to choose options for a meaningful life.

This may lead one to think that Kymlicka is a communitarian but, as already mentioned, he does not think it necessary to give a full-blown communitarian account of the relationship between culture and identity in order to defend the claim that being a member of a culture is a primary good that enables individuals to choose what to do with their lives.

Kymlicka is careful to expand on the idea of culture that he defends as a 'context of choice':

> If we view cultural membership as a primary good within Rawls's scheme of justice, then it is important to remember that it is a good in its capacity of providing meaningful options for us, and aiding our ability to judge for ourselves the value of our life-plans. (1989: 166)

He is wary of loose notions of culture, group or community that tend to endow these collective forms of association with a special 'character' or 'essence'. According to Kymlicka some communitarians, in reacting against strong individualism, have tended to anthropomorphize the idea of culture itself. At the extreme, this is to treat 'a culture' as an agent acting in the social world; but even if cultural communities are often thought to be more important than the individuals who compose them there is a tendency, argues Kymlicka, to endow cultural communities with qualities only really attributable to individual people. Even those communitarians who avoid such problematic claims all too often over-emphasize the intrinsic role culture plays in our identity formation, as if the importance of culture is that we imbibe its character or essence as we grow and mature. Kymlicka steers away from such conceptions of community because he is concerned that they seem to culminate in the claim that any substantial change (that is, a significant change in the character) of a community would amount to a loss of culture for the members of that community. This is simply not the case, according to Kymlicka. It fails to notice, he argues, that cultures often change and that they do so precisely as a result of the choices made by those who belong to the cultural community. A community can change its character (quite substantially indeed) without destroying its actual structure as a meaningful 'context of choice' for the individuals that constitute it. By way of example, he cites the 'Quiet Revolution' that occurred in French Canada in the 1960s, one which witnessed French-Canadians making 'very different choices than they traditionally had done' (167). One might also cite the liberalization of attitudes to sexuality in certain Catholic countries, such as the Republic of Ireland, while 'Irish culture' nonetheless continues to be a crucial source which the Irish draw upon to determine their aims and goals in life, be they 'at home' or part of the world-wide Irish diaspora.

Kymlicka therefore disagrees with the communitarian conception of the self, on the grounds that it overdoes the notion of our attachment to our cultural heritage. To underline this contrast, it is worth considering Kymlicka's position *vis-à-vis* Sandel's claims regarding 'constitutive attachments' (see Chapter 4). For Kymlicka these deep attachments clearly form part of our sense of a meaningful life, and therefore attachment, in the form of membership, is a primary good; but to say they are 'constitutive' of our identity is an overstatement. He maintains that we can radically (that is completely, though perhaps painfully) alter our sense of who we are, where we come from, what is meaningful for us and so on, while still remaining fundamentally the same person. If this is the case, he concludes, then our cultural attachments, important as they are, are not constitutive of our identity in any strong sense of the term. While Kymlicka places a high value upon cultural membership, therefore, his work is still rooted in the individualist tradition of normative political theory. In part, it is this innovative attempt to give culture high priority, while still remaining an individualist, that has brought his ideas to the forefront of contemporary debate in normative political philosophy.

However, the elements of Kymlicka's argument discussed so far only establish that *a* 'context of choice' is important for individuals, in that a cultural background is needed to provide a rich source of values and beliefs that people must draw on in defining their goals in life. The problem this raises is that, on Kymlicka's analysis, it need not be *our* culture of origin that provides the meaningful context of choice *for us*. It could be argued, therefore, that Kymlicka's retreat from strong communitarian assumptions means his position does not preclude a dominant culture effectively wiping others out by attaining the status of a cultural monopoly. In such circumstances, individuals would still have a context that would give meaning to their choices; but the context would be that of the dominant culture. Kymlicka, noticing the difficulties this creates, rejects the idea that as long as there is a context of choice, it doesn't matter which one. He argues that to generalize in this way would be to legitimate the politics of assimilation that would, *de facto*, result in the gradual eradication of the minority cultures his work set out to defend. His case rests on the claim that it is not just culture in general that gives us a context for meaningful choices, but *our* culture that does so – especially if this culture is under threat. 'People are bound in an important way,' he says, 'to their own cultural community. We can't just transplant people from one culture to another, even if we provide the opportunity to learn the other language and culture' (1989: 175). But in what sense can Kymlicka defend this position, without accepting that our culture provides 'constitutive' attachments that make us the people we are? In which case, the communitarian idea of a cultural character or essence may seem plausible.

Clearly Kymlicka's argument that cultural membership is a primary good does not raise significant issues in homogenous societies. In plural societies, however, it has some very far-reaching consequences. In plural societies members of some cultures may be at a serious disadvantage and they may be justified in demanding special rights to rectify that injustice. Some minority cultures may even be facing extinction unless they obtain special rights to protect them. However, special rights can only be granted, argues Kymlicka, in relation to certain circumstances that disadvantage a minority culture; specifically, circumstances for which they could not be held responsible. Any disadvantage that is the result of choices made by members of a culture is a disadvantage for which the cultural members can legitimately be held responsible, and for which they need not receive any special dispensation in the form of rights. Having argued the case for cultural membership as a primary good, Kymlicka (1995) must now address the complexities of modern social and political life in order to assess the practicalities of assigning rights to individuals as members of certain cultural communities.

A key distinction, for Kymlicka, is the difference between bi- or multi-national countries and polyethnic countries. The former are those countries where more than one group were part of the founding of the nation itself: this includes those countries that have an aboriginal people who were not allowed to be involved in the formation of the nation, such as the USA, Canada, Australia and New Zealand. The latter are societies that include different ethnicities by virtue of the free movement of people. This distinction is invoked to distinguish different cultural groups: for example, comparing the claims of Native Americans and the claims of 'New York Jews' does not help us to sift through the cultural complexity of modern democracies, according to Kymlicka. It is important, he argues, that not all cultural groups should be afforded the same rights to protect their culture as a context of choice. For aboriginal peoples, according to Kymlicka, rights to self-government are fundamental. Regarding polyethnic societies, he argues for a more limited set of rights – narrower in scope, and arising from particular aspects of dominant cultural practices that disadvantage the minority group despite their free movement into the territory. For example, the right to public documents in French in Quebec, or the right to publicly funded media in Gaelic in Scotland, are ways to ensure that these minority cultures are not required to give up their language (which would impose serious restrictions on their culture) in order to take part in public life.

This may appear to be a sensible way to approach the protection of minority cultures, but it does raise some fundamental issues that strike at the heart of the individualist and communitarian versions of liberalism. For instance, should a predominantly liberal culture provide public funds to support the language of a minority culture that oppresses some of its own members? Kymlicka recognizes this difficulty, but tries to draw a line under such problems by arguing that cultural communities are only worthy of protection on the grounds that the culture itself forms a meaningful context of choice for *all* the members of the community. Furthermore, he argues that special rights for minority cultures must be granted only as 'external protections' against dominant hegemonic cultures; they are not to be considered as 'internal restrictions' on the members of a cultural community – or, to the extent that they restrict members such restrictions must be consistent with general liberal principles regarding individual human rights. However, if we consider the rights of women in the context of the multiculturalism debate, we shall see that not all theorists believe Kymlicka's approach to be as liberal, or as convincing, as he thinks it is.

MINORITY CULTURES AND THE RIGHTS OF WOMEN

As the multiculturalism debates have taken centre stage in normative political philosophy over the last two decades, it was noticeable that the participants in the debates paid little attention to the women who constituted half the membership of minority cultures in liberal democratic states. The sense that women were being ignored in these debates was brought to the fore by Susan Moller Okin's (1999) wonderfully titled article: 'Is multiculturalism bad for women?'. Here, Okin argues that the desire to accommodate the claims of different cultures in one political territory by affording certain group rights to minority cultures can lead to the erosion and restriction of the individual rights of the members of the cultural group. In particular, the rights of women could be seriously affected because most, if not all, cultural groups are fundamentally patriarchal in structure and ideology. To defend the existence of a cultural community is often to defend the existence of the sexual, physical and verbal abuse of women that is sustained by the cultural practices of many communities. The liberal democratic drive to give equal respect to different cultures may be praiseworthy in the abstract, but in reality it is involved in deeply problematic developments in the legal and political institutions of liberal democracies. For example, she cites the 'cultural defences' constructed by lawyers who seek to legitimate rape, violence and oppression of women. Moreover, Kymlicka's attempt to ward off these dangers is deemed inadequate on the grounds that 'discrimination against and control of the freedom of females are practised, to a greater or lesser extent, by virtually all cultures, past and present' (1999: 21). She continues:

> Although Kymlicka rightly objects, then, to the granting of group rights to minority cultures that practise overt sex discrimination, his arguments for multiculturalism fail to register what he himself acknowledges elsewhere: that the subordination of women is often informal and private, and that virtually no culture in the world today, minority or majority, could pass his 'no sex discrimination' test if it were applied in the private sphere. (1999: 22)

Nonetheless, Okin concludes cautiously: 'Unless women – and more specifically, young women (since older women often are co-opted into reinforcing gender inequality) – are fully represented in negotiations about group rights, their interests may be harmed rather than promoted by the granting of such rights' (1999: 24). From this perspective, the desire to recognize culture as valuable for individuals would appear to be damaging the very human rights, especially those of women, which have been so hard-won in the preceding centuries. But this gives rise to a related question: how universal are the human rights to which Okin is appealing? The next section addresses this issue through the lens of feminism, and considers the debates about identity that dominated the second-wave feminist movement of the 1960s and 70s.

WOMEN, CULTURE AND IDENTITY

Are there essential features of being a woman that unite women across cultures, classes, sexualities and races that should provide the bedrock of feminist analyses? Are women defined as much, or even more so, by their race, sexuality, culture and class as they are defined by their 'woman-ness'? What happens to feminist politics (in theory and practice) if there is nothing essential that is shared by women of different classes, cultures, races and sexualities? While it is commonplace to characterize feminists as concerned with debates about whether or not women and men are fundamentally the same or different (the sameness/difference debates), much of the interesting feminist work of recent decades has emerged from the question of whether or not women are essentially the same or irreducibly different from *each other* – usually called the essentialism/anti-essentialism debate. The rise of this debate within feminism is a complicated story, but three overlapping factors seem particularly important in explaining why so many feminists came to see the idea of 'woman' as inherently problematic.

The first factor is the implosion of second-wave feminism. The history of feminism is usually seen as a series of 'waves'. First-wave feminism had female suffrage as its main focal point, and was expressed in the writings of Mary Wollstonecraft, Harriet Taylor, Virginia Woolf and others. The feminists of the first wave argued that women should be given equal access to the public sphere, especially through the extension to women of the right to vote. After women had gained the vote in many Western countries, there was a move beyond the broadly liberal feminism of the first wave. Feminists began to focus on the fact that simply having the right to vote did not bring equality for women. Consequently, feminists began to investigate the various areas of women's oppression: the house, the workplace, the bedroom, the culture and, last but not least, the mind. Feminism had entered a new era, produced a second wave, as it turned to the analysis of the numerous ways in which women were oppressed in different spheres of their own lives, and analysed the complications of different women seeming to be differently oppressed, depending on the particular contexts of their lives. The result was a series of debates about which form of oppression 'matters most' – that is, which factor is most fundamental in maintaining the inequality of women in society. For example, are women oppressed, first and foremost, in the workplace *as women* or as *working-class* women? Indeed, the tension between Marxist feminists (such as Firestone and Rowbotham) and the rest of the women's movement was a key early indicator that feminists would struggle to unite around a clear idea of what it is to be a woman. While it was agreed that women were oppressed, and that oppression in the workplace was central to the general subordination of women, there were intense debates regarding whether or not patriarchy would disappear if capitalism was overcome. Similar debates crystallized around sexuality and race. The sexuality debates, which gained much of the public attention, focused on questions of lesbianism: will women only free themselves from the sexual oppression of men through lesbianism? Are lesbian sexual practices more in tune with women's sexuality, and do they enable women to experience their sexuality as liberating rather than subsumed within dominant patriarchal desires? The spark that lit the race and gender debates was the growing realization that feminism was often a pursuit of liberal-minded white women who took it on themselves to speak for women everywhere. As non-white feminists found their voice, it became clear that speaking on behalf of others was a feature of the patriarchal structures of society that feminists were objecting to – yet this feature was being replicated within feminism itself. Eventually, it became difficult to see what united a working-class heterosexual black woman from Atlanta with a middle-class lesbian lawyer studying at Cambridge, or a Sudanese Muslim peasant woman. So second-wave feminism began to implode as close analysis revealed the significant differences between individual women.

The second factor that led to the essentialism/anti-essentialism debates within feminism was the arrival on the intellectual scene of general philosophical critiques of essence. Feminism, like all critical perspectives, has never existed in a vacuum: it always responds and contributes to the latest theoretical developments. Arguably, one of the most profound philosophical developments of the last 40 years has been a sustained critique of the idea of essence. Paradigmatically, we can locate the general critique of essence on three fronts (though, in reality, the picture is much more complicated than this): deconstruction, poststructuralism and postmodernism. First, the late 1960s saw the publication of three books by Jacques Derrida (English translations appeared in 1973, 1974 and 1978) that ushered into the intellectual world the idea of deconstruction. 'Deconstruction' was a term coined by Derrida to express a form of critical practice aimed at exposing the inevitable gaps or lacunae that both structure and de-structure any text; hence de-con-struction is both de-structuring the text to find how it is held together and con-structing an interpretation of the text that shows how the structure holding it together is never watertight, on its own terms; that is, that it has no essence. Just to ward off an obvious rejoinder, it is important to mention that the text that is deconstructed is not simply a written text or speech but any 'discursive practice'; patriarchal behaviour, for example, is a social text that can be deconstructed. Secondly, deconstruction is often considered to be part of a broader intellectual movement called poststructuralism, but because of the influence of Derrida's ideas on feminism it is worth separating it out. Poststructuralism, as the name suggests, is a theoretical position that emerged after the structuralist revolution in linguistics, sociology and psychoanalysis. In short, it is an attempt to radicalize the structuralist critique of humanism by arguing that the underlying structures that shape our sense of ourselves – cultural systems, economic apparatuses, psychological theories, and the social sciences – are fluid and changeable rather than fixed and timeless. This sense of fluidity as a move away from underlying essences is also characteristic of the third major critique of essence, postmodernism. In the famous formulation of Jean-Francois Lyotard, postmodernism is the de-legitimization of the grand narratives of modernism (historical progress, the triumph of reason, the forward march of civilization) and, in place of these narratives, the valorization of playful excess, contingency and difference. Feminists saw in these philosophical assaults on the idea of essence ways of formulating critiques of the idea of 'woman'. Moreover, many feminists saw in deconstruction, poststructuralism and postmodernism a series of breaks with (patriarchal) intellectual traditions that could be harnessed to provide alternative concepts and categories within feminism. They suggested that the formulation of a new language of feminism was possible: one that was able to express the differences between women, their lack of shared essential characteristics, but one that could nonetheless retain a spirit of criticism.

Closely allied to these intellectual movements were the economic and social developments that have come to be known as *globalization*. Until the 1970s, the vast majority of feminist activity and theorizing had taken place in the educational institutions and and on the streets of the Western world. Even as second-wave feminists came to see that feminism must move beyond the domains of middle-class liberal white women, it still tended to concentrate on the experiences of Western women. It is only very recently that feminism has really begun to grapple with the experiences of women from all over the world. This brings differences – especially differences of race, religion and culture – to the fore, and has led some feminists to question whether or not there is a model of female oppression that can be applied across cultural boundaries. For example, are feminists in the Indian sub-continent (fundamentally) fighting the same forms of oppression that feminists in Brazil are fighting?

This question is typical of a debate within feminism as feminists try to answer the question: who are we? An excellent example of the issues at stake in this debate is an exchange that took place between Okin (1994) and another feminist theorist, Jane Flax (1995). In brief, Okin's argument is two-fold. On the one hand, she takes issue with anti-essentialist feminists on the grounds that they deploy theories of difference in ways that neglect empirical evidence of shared inequalities and that are inherently problematic in themselves, because they cannot prevent feminism sliding into relativism. On the other hand, she proposes that a theory of justice, if properly informed by feminist insights, can be developed that will be able to express the common problems facing all women regardless of culture (or, to say the same thing in a different way, a theory of justice can be universal but remain sensitive to cultural differences between women). Interestingly, the theory of justice that she promotes, in its modified feminist version, is Rawls' from *A Theory of Justice* (see Chapter 4). As already noted, Rawls invented the idea of the 'veil of ignorance' as a device for constructing the principles that will guide a fair society, because it embodies the features of a neutral, moral, point of view. The contractors, in not knowing who they are, are forced to think as if they could be anyone. Although Rawls had to revise his theory to include gender as a feature that would be placed behind the veil of ignorance, once this is taken in to account the case is straightforward, for Okin. After all, 'what man would endorse gross genital mutilation not knowing whose genitals?'(1994: 20). Similarly, what woman would sanction such a practice, not knowing the cultural background that they will have once the veil is lifted? Rawls' device, therefore, provides a test that allows us to sift out the universal oppressions from the cultural sensitivities. Okin accepts that differences are important but argues that they are not essential, and she advocates a universal theory of justice to ground feminist political theory. Talking of the various oppressions that women suffer around the world, she says: 'the issue is not so much different as "similar but more so"' (1994: 8). Okin's emphasis on oppression is, in part, her attempt to stay a step removed from the philosophical pitfalls of the essentialism/anti-essentialism debate. Nonetheless, her response to the question 'who are we (women)?' is unequivocal: 'we are those people who are oppressed *as women*'.

In response, Flax argues that Okin's construction of a shared form of women's oppression is to obscure, colonize and distort the experiences of women in different contexts. She also argues that Okin mistakenly sees race and class as elements that can be suspended from discussions of gender inequality, when in fact women are constituted as much by their class position and racial background as they are by their gender. Flax argues that 'gender is always raced, and race is always gendered' (1995: 505), and any feminist analysis that neglects race is implicitly assuming a problematic 'white' perspective. The way forward, she claims, is 'an ethic of difference', because this is the only context-sensitive way of applying the idea of justice. As Flax puts it: 'a homogenous dominance/oppression model cannot account for the complicated and contradictory constitution of gender' (1995: 501). Flax's arguments neatly summarize the anti-essentialist position within feminism, and thus provide a (sort of) definitive answer to the guiding question of this chapter: 'who are we (women)?' feminists ask; 'we (women) are all different,' Flax replies.

One of the issues that divides Okin and Flax most severely is the role of the 'distanced critic' that Okin advocates as necessary in situations where women have come to internalize the oppression against them. For Okin, it is clear that being a white, middle-class feminist is not the issue when it comes to arguing against cultural practices that offend against women's basic human rights, such as female genital mutilation. Even if one is 'distanced' from the cultural practice that one is criticizing, Okin argues, one can still justifiably claim that it is a form of abuse and oppression and one should, therefore, as a feminist, seek to intervene, for example by protesting. Flax sees this as deeply problematic. For her, the only justifiable position of the critic is an *internal* one. The critic must understand the issues fully and can only do this by being inside the cultural context that explains the practice itself. It is only then, for Flax, that the real issues will emerge, rather than those issues being potentially hidden behind a banner proclaiming the universal oppression of sexism. Underneath the question of who we (women) are is this issue of who is the (legitimate) critic who really separates them. The next two sections present some attempts to go beyond this dichotomy of being a critic on the inside or a critic from the outside.

THE FUSION OF HORIZONS

Having brought to the surface some of the feminist claims that animate debates surrounding culture and critique, it is worth returning to the canvas of liberal democratic theory to see if we can paint an alternative picture of how cultural identity can, even must, be the subject of criticism, and yet also can, and must, be the source from which critical interventions draw their force. As we have seen, one of the great challenges of multicultural liberal democracies is that of recognizing and respecting different cultural identities within one constitutional state. As Amy Guttman asks if there can be 'a politics of recognition that respects a multitude of multicultural identities and does not script too tightly any one life?' (1994: xi). The idea of a politics of recognition was developed by Charles Taylor as his response to the difficulties associated with traditional liberal concerns about the relationship between culture and identity.

For Taylor, many of the problems that surround cultural politics can be traced back to the way we make 'judgements of worth'. What he calls 'difference-blind' liberals tend to assume that the only moral point of view is a culturally neutral one. Multiculturalists, on the other hand, assume that the only legitimate way of judging the worth of culture is from inside it. Taylor argues that both of these positions assume that there is 'an ultimate horizon' from which to make judgements of worth about different cultures. In contrast, he argues that no such ultimate horizon exists, and that the best we can have is the complex negotiation of 'our' horizon with that of the 'other' culture that we are trying to judge. In this way, the judgements of worth that underpin multicultural and global politics cannot be simply formulated; they must depend on a fusion of horizons. As Taylor puts it:

The 'fusion of horizons' operates through our developing new vocabularies of comparison, by means of which we can articulate these contrasts. So that if and when we can ultimately find substantive support for our initial presumption, it is on the basis of an understanding of what constitutes worth that we couldn't possibly have had at the beginning. We have reached the judgment partly by transforming our standards. (1994: 67)

If we approach our own and other cultures with openness to fusing the insights of both we can, according to Taylor, find a new basis for criticism, not just of other cultures but also *of our own*. The core to reaching this fusion of horizons is to presume, in the first instance, that every culture is of equal worth. Rather than prejudge the issue of worth by presuming an internal or external perspective on cultural critique, Taylor argues, we should always begin by assuming that every culture, at least every culture that has stood the test of time, must be thought to contain elements that express fundamental human needs and that would, therefore, enrich our own. Addressing the question of what features of the world could guarantee a basis for such equal respect, Taylor says:

. . . on the human level, one could argue that it is reasonable to suppose that cultures that have provided the horizon of meaning for large numbers of human beings, of diverse characters and temperaments, over a long period of time – that have, in other words, articulated their sense of the good, the holy, the admirable – are almost certainly to have something that deserves our admiration and respect, even if it is accompanied by much that we have to abhor and reject. Perhaps one could put it another way: it would take a supreme arrogance to discount this possibility a priori. (1994: 72–3)

To recognize this and to engage with others on the basis of fusing our cultural horizons with theirs is to promote, according to Taylor, a truly liberal dialogue with others that responds to the demands of contemporary identity politics. That said, it seems right to ask if Taylor's hope of the fusion of cultural horizons is just that, a hope, rather than a worked-out political solution to a problem at the heart of liberal democracies. Perhaps Habermas's more thoroughgoing account of exactly what is at stake in dialogue may suggest an alternative approach, or a complementary one that nonetheless secures Taylor's hope more firmly.

INTERSUBJECTIVITY AND THE POLITICS OF RECOGNITION

Habermas (1994) is sympathetic to Taylor's claim that difference-blind liberalism in fact legitimizes *not* recognizing people's cultural identity, and that this lack of recognition may, in certain circumstances, constitute a form of harm against the individual. Where he departs from Taylor is with the suggestion that we must rethink the nature of liberal claims, that a politics of recognition substantially different from a rights-based form of liberalism is required. For Habermas, the resources exist within traditional rights-based versions of difference-blind liberalism to actually recognize cultural identities, and to do so in ways that put people's claims on a more secure footing than the fusion of horizons. Nonetheless, for these resources to be excavated from within liberalism, liberals must undergo a kind of paradigm shift by reconstructing the idea of personal identity on the basis of our relationships with each other, rather than on ideas of individual autonomy: on an inter-subjective rather than a subjective model of autonomy. As Habermas claims:

A correctly understood theory of rights requires a politics of recognition that protects the integrity of the individual in the life contexts in which his or her identity is formed. This does not require an alternative model that would correct the individualistic design of the system of rights through other normative perspectives. All that is required is the consistent actualisation of the system of rights. (1994: 113)

It has already been noted (Chapter 5) that Habermas diagnosed subjectivism as one of the key causes of the sicknesses that have debilitated the Enlightenment project. In line with this general claim, Habermas argues that the contemporary dilemmas surrounding the politics of cultural recognition in contemporary liberal states are also symptomatic of a failure to see the real intersubjective basis of our identity. Once the dialogical basis of our identity is understood correctly, then we will be able to formulate the 'consistent articulation of a system of rights' required to secure both individual rights and cultural identity: 'when properly understood, the theory of rights is by no means blind to cultural differences' (1994: 112). The central idea that Habermas's draws on is that:

> [T]hose to whom the law is addressed can acquire autonomy . . . only to the extent that they can understand themselves to be the authors of the laws to which they are subject as private legal persons . . . For in the final analysis, private legal persons cannot even attain the enjoyment of equal individual liberties unless they themselves, by jointly exercising their autonomy as citizens, arrive at a clear understanding about what interests and criteria are justified and in what respects equal things will be treated equally and unequal things unequally in any particular case. (1994: 112–13)

Superficially, this is not dissimilar to Taylor's call for a fusion of horizons. However, the crux of the matter is that Habermas is arguing that the recognition Taylor rightly sees as so central to democratic life is already contained within the liberal ideal of individual autonomy, if that autonomy is construed as the product of a collective self-authorship – by which is meant that each individual becomes autonomous (that is, the author of their own destiny) only by virtue of being able to exercise that autonomy in the context of being part of the law-making process. Deliberative democracies (Chapter 5), if properly constituted, already contain the necessary mechanisms for this to happen, while also securing rights for individuals as individuals. Therefore, there is no need for Taylor to argue that we must presuppose the equal worth of every cultural formation, because what is really at stake is the equal worth of every individual as a democratic citizen participating in the construction of the laws that govern their behaviour. Although these individuals bring their cultural baggage with them, it would be unwise, argues Habermas, to assume that it is the baggage that is worthy of respect, when in fact it is the citizen him or herself who is worthy of respect. Taking this to its obvious conclusion, whereas Taylor's argument presumes that cultural formations should be preserved because they contain elements worthy to all of us, Habermas argues that cultures should not be artificially sustained if the members of those cultures do not themselves sustain them as they engage in democratic deliberation. Habermas claims that it is wrong to think of cultural forms as being in need of a 'kind of preservation of species by administrative means' (1994: 130). In effect, we have come back to a position that is close to Kymlicka's idea that cultures are only important to the extent that they provide individuals with frameworks that enable autonomy to flourish. So the fundamentally important figure within the cultural identity debates must remain the individual, for Habermas as for Kymlicka. The difference between them is that while Kymlicka argues that a Rawlsian definition of primary goods can do the work of securing just the correct extent of rights to cultural membership, Habermas argues that this task must be achieved by a fully functioning deliberative democracy, because it is through rationally motivated deliberation that identity is formed. In the next and concluding chapter, the normative presumptions underpinning these debates will be challenged and, in the process, it will prove necessary to aim at a definition of political philosophy that rejects some of our standard assumptions about this discipline.

CHAPTER 7

CONCLUSION: IDENTITY, DIFFERENCE AND POLITICAL PHILOSOPHY

In the opening passages of *The Politics* Aristotle argues that the *polis* emerges naturally as human associations develop and expand: from the 'essential' pairing of male and female, to the household which is formed when men rule over women and slaves, to the village that emerges as sons and grandsons set up their own households and, in the end, 'the final association, formed of several villages, is the *polis*' (1989: 59). As the *polis* is 'the final association', the form of association that is not superseded, then it is the culmination of human nature, for 'whatever is the end-product of the coming into existence of any object, that is what we call its nature' (1981: 59). Aristotle's famous quote follows directly from the reasoning: 'man is by nature a political animal' (1989: 59). In fact, in today's language we should think of this as meaning that 'man is by nature an ethical, social and political animal', because Aristotle's idea of the *polis* was much broader than the connotations we today associate with politics or 'the state' (as *polis* is often translated, anachronistically). This also explains Aristotle's development of the argument as he distinguishes the collective life of humans from that of bees, on the grounds that human beings 'alone have perception of good and evil, just and unjust etc. It is the sharing of a common view in these matters that makes a household and a *polis*' (1981: 60). In other words, the culmination of 'man's' nature is to be found in the realization of a polity that all *men* agree is just, rather than in an instrumental association based on self-interest.

Human nature, politics and justice are all tightly wrapped up in a series of foundational claims that have profoundly shaped political philosophy for millennia. Thinking back to the social contract tradition, for all the differences between Hobbes and Aristotle (he was, after all, an explicitly anti-Aristotelian thinker), we still find in Hobbes a set of foundational claims about human nature that dictate the nature of political activity, and secure within that an explanation of justice as whatever the sovereign decides is just. In a contemporary variant on the same theme, Rawls' political philosophy follows a similar pattern: a set of minimal assumptions about human nature that give rise to a particular view of the nature of political associations, which then inform his theory of justice. Moreover, though there are plenty of alternatives to Rawls' presumptions about identity that challenge his individualist presuppositions (even to the extent, in the work of Habermas for example, of providing an alternative framework for conceptualizing human autonomy), the approach, the structure of argumentation and the aims remain fundamentally the same as those articulated by Aristotle two millennia earlier. Undoubtedly, the wording of claims has been reworked extensively to the point where they are rigorously nuanced and technically precise, but the underlying questions, the basic terms of reference and the foundational assumptions about human identity remain. It is this undercurrent of similarity that, in part, defines the nature of political philosophy, at least as conceived within the Anglo-American normative mainstream. Although political philosophers are prone to create major schematic divisions between different schools of thought, these are, more often than not, straightforward disagreements between philosophers working within the same basic conceptual territory. Is this because political philosophy must be done in this way: must it begin with a claim about human nature, work up to a claim about the nature of politics, and then conclude with a theory of justice (or liberty, equality, democracy)? Or can political philosophy be 'done differently'; by which I mean, can it begin with assumptions that prioritize difference rather than nature and identity?

A good place to start is with the difference feminists, not least because of Aristotle's extremely dubious claims about women – claims that have echoed through the history of political philosophy down to the present. In the last chapter, Flax was introduced as a feminist ill at ease with foundational claims about 'woman' that tended to mask a bias towards white, Western, middle-class, heterosexual women. In this chapter, some of the philosophical lineage that informs her work will be explored by way of a discussion of the three leading figures of 'French feminism': Luce Irigaray, Julia Kristeva and Hélène Cixous.

By exploring the ways in which these writers have brought identity (in particular the identity of women) into question, we can also explore how they conceive the task of a critically oriented philosophical practice that prioritizes difference. This will bring insight into how we may think about political philosophy outside the normative mainstream, and expose the problems presented by trying to step outside this mainstream.

FRENCH FEMINIST CRITIQUES OF IDENTITY

Recognizing the problematic nature of such a move, there is merit in treating Irigaray, Kristeva and Cixous as indicative of a general approach within feminist (political) philosophy usually labelled 'French feminism'. The main reason that these three have been, and continue to be, lumped together as the paradigmatic figures of French feminism is that they all had (different) relations with the group 'Psychanalyse et Politique' (often referred to as 'Psych et Po', and later renamed 'Politique et Psychanalyse'). This group was instrumental, through its publishing arm *des femmes*, in getting their work published and translated into English. In the Anglo-American feminist imagination, therefore, these three came to symbolize the project that was labelled, partly as a term of abuse by liberal feminists, 'French feminism'. Certainly, each of the three has developed a body of work that is extremely complex (though not necessarily obscure), multidimensional, and politically and philosophically challenging. But, at the risk of oversimplification, we can establish the major contribution of each in terms that show significant overlapping concerns within their theoretical analyses, if we relate their work to what we may identify as 'the roots' of French feminism. Three figures are especially important in this regard: Simone de Beauvoir, Jacques Lacan and Jacques Derrida.

De Beauvoir's *The Second Sex* is central to the development of feminism because in it she argued that women were not just politically and materially oppressed by men, but also categorized and defined in ways that meant the very idea of being a 'woman' could only be understood as 'the other' in relation to the already masculine definitions of what it is to be a human subject. In short, according to de Beauvoir, because the idea of 'man' has been used to define what it is to be human, women are (psychologically, intellectually and existentially) already less than human, such that a woman's sense of herself always contains this feeling of lack. This sense of being 'the other' therefore prevents women from developing the capacity for self-realization. Moreover, it obscures women's view of how they might 'transcend' the situations that masculine society has created for them: housewife, mother, lover, and so on. A woman, according to de Beauvoir, is routinely denied access to herself, to her 'immanent' self. Nonetheless, de Beauvoir's analysis, informed as it was by an existentialist philosophy, contained a 'utopian' hope. Women, she argued, could realize their own sense of self by working on the transcendence of their otherness: that is, through the ongoing labour of giving meaning to their own lives rather than falling into the predefined categories that men have established for women over centuries of increasingly subtle oppression. By way of this radical activity of claiming their identity for themselves, women could become what they wanted to be, rather than simply act out what men wanted them to be. For the generation of French feminists following de Beauvoir this vision of the liberation of women through the act of claiming an identity for themselves was generally accepted, but with a couple of significant twists. On the one hand, later feminists tended to celebrate rather than lament women's otherness as it was argued that celebration situated 'the feminine' as a *privileged* critical perspective on masculine norms of human nature and subjectivity. Her successors were also more sceptical than de Beauvoir with regard to the possibility of transcending otherness, as they feared that this desire for self-realization would amount to the return of a masculine ideal. Instead, later feminists (in the French tradition especially) tended to argue that being 'the other' gives women the chance to explore radically new ways of being in the world.

A second great influence on Irigaray, Kristeva and Cixous was the psychoanalytical theorist, Jacques Lacan (1977). Lacan is primarily known for his structuralist interpretation of Freudian psychoanalysis. Structuralism is a critique of humanism which treats human identity as defined and structured by language, signs, roles and rituals which underpin social relations. Lacan referred to this underlying social structure as the 'symbolic order', and argued that to be a functioning person within any given society one must 'enter into' that society's symbolic order: if one does not achieve this, for whatever reason, then a variety of psychological disorders result. Rather than see the Oedipal drama as acted out by individuals, Lacan interpreted it as part of the basic constitution of society itself. The problem for women, therefore, is that this symbolic order is constituted by masculine signs ('human' means the same as 'man'), and this means women do not have an adequate system of signs and symbols their own language, for instance – to express themselves as women (which may explain why women's attempts to express themselves *as women* are often treated as a kind of hysteria). French feminists both took on board Lacan's insights, and transformed them in various ways. In general, though, one of the elements that unite French feminists is their desire to explore ways in which women can find a means of expressing themselves in a social order that orients all language and thought around phallic concepts and categories. Given that political philosophy as a discipline and social practice is, on this account, part of the phallic symbolic order, it was suggested that political philosophy must be transformed, in terms of its basic concepts and argumentative presumptions, if it is to give voice to women's experience of living in a masculine world and bring substance to women's hope of transforming that world.

A third key influence on French feminism is Jacques Derrida (see Chapter 6). One of the problems with Lacan's thinking, and structuralism in general, is that it offers limited guidance as to how the structures that make us who we are could be different (there is little thought given, for example, to explaining the changing nature of the symbolic order). Derrida can be said to offer an account of how every linguistic order is always already incomplete in itself, and because of this incompleteness, it is subject to rupture and change. As such, the symbolic order can be deconstructed (see Chapter 6). French feminists saw in the deconstructive method a way of expressing the situation of women without committing the feminist project to the problematic, masculine, idea of 'transcendence' that animated de Beauvoir's utopian vision. In other words, they saw how they could challenge masculine language and thought from a position which is immanent, or internal to the symbolic order itself. Turning to each of the three major figures of French feminism, we can see how they developed these general themes in their own particular ways.

Irigaray is perhaps best known for her argument that there is a masculine core running through the history of philosophy. This masculine core is found in the way that the philosophical tradition constantly returns to identity and sameness, thereby negating any sustained account of what it is to be different, and excluding 'woman' in its very construction. In *Speculum of the Other Woman* (1985a), for example, she uses a clinical image to convey this: it is as if philoso-phers have tried to understand 'woman' by inserting a speculum into the idea of woman, which only reflects the male gaze back at itself. But for her, the task of 'philosophy in the feminine' is to reject the very idea of sameness as masculine, and to explore the realms of difference. In particular, she argues that difference should be understood as that which is utterly different, rather than as a difference essentially re-appropriated within an overarching idea of the same: it is some-times said that in Christian terms men and women are different but both expressions of God's will, that is, expressions of an ultimate guarantor of identity between two superficially different sexes. In developing a philosophy of the feminine, Irigaray argues that women should explore their own bodies to search for a language of difference. In contrast to the phallic construction of sameness (ultimately, Irigaray argues, the phallus represents the 'one truth', linear and hierarchical, to which masculine thinkers aspire) she envisions a 'labial' notion of difference. Irigaray argues that the 'two lips' of the labia are in fact 'neither one nor two' and that this 'keeps woman in touch with her-self, but without any possibility of distinguishing what is touching from what is touched' (1985b: 32). A women's language of difference, in other words, need not presuppose the masculine distinctions of subject and object, perceiver and perceived, or other dichotomous conceptual pairs. As Irigaray (1985b) says: '"She" is indefinitely other in herself', and therefore 'she' is both 'one and many', 'universal and particular', and so forth.

Kristeva (1986) develops a similar account of woman's potential, but she does so primarily through the framework of psychoanalysis. She broadly accepts the Freudian narrative of child development as presented through Lacan's structuralism, but she draws out an aspect of the way children develop language that, she argues, has been over-looked by these masculine authors. In particular, she argues that there is a phase between birth and entry into the symbolic order that she calls the semiotic. With a literal (perhaps too literal) rendering of this phase, it can be thought of as the babbling of the child before it enters the world of language (a phase my mother describes as the time when babies 'tell stories'). This pre-Oedipal stage is marked by the playful use of sounds, a kind of nonsensical invention, and a delight in the texture of words rather than in their meaning. This playfulness is usually curtailed as children enter the world of the symbolic order where sounds must be attached to words, and words to things, experiences and so on; but, Kristeva argues, the semiotic aspect of language is never entirely lost. Indeed, it is retained within the symbolic order and it is this retention of the semiotic babbling that explains the possibility of creative, indeed revolutionary, uses of language – and therefore new ways of thinking about the world. Interestingly, and problematically for some commentators, the writers that she thinks most clearly express and embody the semiotic dimension of language within their work are predominantly male: Samuel Beckett and James Joyce, for instance. Kristeva's 'feminism', therefore, is largely about embracing the critical possibilities inherent in the creative deployment of language – though she is hostile to the idea that only women are capable of this. As she says, 'The belief that "one is a woman" is almost as absurd and obscurantist as the belief that "one is a man"'(1981: 137). Nonetheless, for those feminists who see the need to crack open the symbolic order if women are to find their own sense of self, Kristeva's work holds up the hope that language contains within itself the tools for a revolution in the symbolic order. Not all feminists would agree, but if one is to challenge the ways in which women's identities have been constructed by masculine discourses then dislodging the very idea of symbolic identity may be the most revolutionary activity of all.

As regards the last of our three French feminists, Cixous is most well known for her development and deployment of *l'écriture féminine*, a feminine form of writing that challenges the binary logic of traditional masculine approaches to writing (*littérature*). On the face of it, this sounds directly opposed to Kristeva's claims that the revolutionary potential of language is not specifically gendered. This is not the case, though, as Cixous also argues that the task is to write in 'the feminine', not necessarily 'as a woman'. Indeed, she believes it is perfectly possible for men to write in the feminine and also turns to arch-modernists such as Beckett and Joyce to show how language can become feminine. Interestingly, it was her analysis of the overarching binary oppositions that structure all masculine philosophical, literary, psychoanalytical and cultural texts that led her to conceive of a more plural, expressive and expansive style which she considered to be feminine. In a famous literary and philosophical critique, Cixous asks 'Where is she?' in the following binary oppositions that recur throughout literary classics: 'Activity/Passivity, Sun/Moon, Culture/Nature, Day/Night, Father/Mother, Head/Heart, Intelligible/Sensitive, Logos/Pathos', and finally 'man/woman'. It is clear, she says, that

'Thought has always worked through opposition . . . by dual, hierarchized oppositions' (1981a: 90). In the language of literature which expresses the languages of life, Cixous argues, we find again and again that women are presented as the passive yet unruly, natural yet sensitive, dark yet emotional creatures who stand in opposition and subordination to men who are characterized by activity, intelligence, logic and so on. In the face of such hierarchical oppositions, Cixous argues, 'Woman must write her self' (1981b: 245) by embracing a feminine form of writing. It is tempting to ask 'what is feminine writing?' However, the question is problematic because it is masculine in its construction, searching as it is for a fixed answer and a single identity, where there may not be one but many different answers and identities. The task of *l'ecriture feminine*, according to Cixous, is to write for oneself in all one's plurality, fending off the masculine desire for a single definitive statement of who we are in favour of a more feminine desire for expansiveness and openness.

While French feminism is a problematic label for many reasons, there are certain common features shared by (at least) these three influential contemporary philosophers. They share a structuralist understanding of how masculine identity has come to be enshrined at all levels of our life, from the most intimate to most public, but they also share a *post*structuralist understanding of how the excluded feminine voice can find a position from which to critique masculine structures of power embedded in the symbolic order. Moreover, French feminists share the view that the critique of masculine structures can enable women to experience life differently, though they are reticent and cautious about the extent to which this critique will lead to women's 'emancipation'. Lastly, although all these theorists seek to explore and re-evaluate the position of 'the feminine' in society, they try to develop nuanced theories of the relationship between gender and sex. If this is the future of feminism – a possibility that is highly contested, not least by other feminists – then what would it mean to construct a feminine future for political philosophy? Is it possible that political philosophy could embrace radical critiques of identity that think beyond human nature, the polity and justice? In truth, it is not only possible, it is already being done. In the next section, we will see how far the critique of identity can (and should?) be taken if political philosophy is to treat difference as pure difference: that is, as a term that is not subordinate to foundational claims about human identity. The focus is Judith Butler's challenging and innovative work on the sex/gender distinction.

THE TROUBLE WITH GENDER

It is time to consider the possibility that the most intimate and 'biological' aspects of our identities are more political than we might think. It is time to talk about sex. To what extent, if any, is our identity as a being of a certain sex, with a given sexuality, a political issue? Clearly, Aristotle presumed that all humans naturally divide into two sexes and that the primary form of human association was that of male and female, mainly for the purpose of reproduction. Given that claims about sex and sexuality play such a foundational role for Aristotle, and also his status within the canon of political philosophy, then we have *prima facie* reasons for subjecting sex and sexuality to political investigation. Just as subsequent political philosophers have queried the presumptions he made about slaves, it may be time for political analysis of his guiding presuppositions regarding sexual difference and sexuality.

Judith Butler's book *Gender Trouble: Feminism and the Subversion of Identity* is one of the principal sources in a growing movement within political philosophy to question such traditional assumptions of sex/gender and sexuality. She wrote this in order to expose the often unconsidered assumptions that feminists (in particular) make about the nature of gender and its relation to sex and sexuality. Butler questions two ideas commonly found within feminism: (a) that sex is natural, given, fixed, unchanging and a-historical, and gender is cultural, contextual, changeable and mutable; and, (b) that sex 'gives rise to' gender in a variety of ways such that it is more or less 'inevitable' that males will be masculine and females will be feminine. Her aim is to 'make trouble' with these assumptions and show that there are other ways of thinking about the relationship between sex and gender. As part of this analysis she also calls into question another assumption: namely, that heterosexuality is the natural and therefore normal mode of sexuality from which others are abnormal deviations. In constructing her alternative analysis of sex/gender/sexuality, Butler relies heavily on Foucault's insights into the disciplinary nature of power (see Chapter 3). Butler applies Foucauldian concepts to the idea of 'woman': in particular, she argues that feminism has often uncritically used this category and not sufficiently considered that invoking the idea of 'woman' (in demanding 'women's rights', for example) may be replicating the discursive practices of the masculine norms which feminists seek to challenge and undermine. As Foucault argued with regard to the sexual liberation discourse of the 1960s, calling for the representation and liberation of women may be dangerous because it implicates 'women' in the masculine world of fixed identities and structures:

> It is not enough to inquire into how women might become more fully represented in language and politics. Feminist critique ought also to understand how the category of 'women', the subject of feminism, is produced and restrained by the very structures of power through which emancipation is sought. (1999: 5)

And:

> If there is a fear that, by no longer being able to take for granted the subject, its gender, its sex, or its materiality, feminism will founder, it might be wise to consider the political consequences of keeping in their place the very premises that have tried to secure our subordination from the start. (1992: 19)

More significantly, however, Butler uses Foucault's insight into how discourses produce complex identities to question the idea that we are naturally sexed beings. Rather than simply assume that sex is a biological phenomenon that resides beyond discourse, Butler draws on Foucault's ideas to argue that our understanding of 'sex' as existing outside social texts and practices is a belief produced by our discourses of sex/gender and sexuality. In *Discipline and Punish*, Foucault argues that 'the body is . . . directly involved in a political field; power relations have an immediate hold upon it; they invest it, train it, torture it, force it, to carry out tasks, to perform ceremonies, to emit signs . . .' (1977: 25). In *Gender Trouble*, Butler argues similarly that the sexed body is not something outside disciplinary power relations; rather, the sexed body is directly implicated in a whole array of regulative practices. Even if the biological body is construed as existing at the very limit of what may be called the political, according to Butler, it is – by virtue of being at the limit – included in political discourses. She argues that:

gender is not to culture as sex is to nature; gender is also the dis-cursive/cultural means by which 'sexed nature' or 'a natural sex' is produced and established as 'prediscursive', prior to culture, a politically neutral surface on which culture acts . . . [This is the] construction of 'sex' as the radically unconstructed. (1999: 11)

The claim here is that the apparently 'biological' and therefore non-political categories of sexual difference (male and female) are in fact constituted, constructed and produced just as are the categories of gender difference – masculine and feminine. If both sex and gender are constructed, however, it does not make sense to talk of sex 'giving rise to' gender; for instance, there is nothing natural, according to Butler, about women, as sexed beings, being nurturing – a culturally gendered aspect of identity. It makes more sense to say that in the political constitution of gender, sex is also brought into being. In fact, gender divisions substantiate the idea of sexual difference as that which *we think* is the basis of our gendered nature! In Butler's words:

It would make no sense, then, to define gender as the cultural interpretation of sex, if sex itself is a gendered category. Gender ought not to be conceived merely as the cultural inscription of meaning on a pre-given sex . . . gender must also designate the very apparatus of production whereby the sexes themselves are established. (1999: 11)

If Butler is right that gender determines sex, and that gender produces our sense of ourselves as sexed beings, then how does this happen? According to her, gender is 'the repeated stylisation of the body, a set of repeated acts within a highly rigid, regulatory frame that congeal over time to produce the appearance of a substance, of a natural sort of being' (1999: 43–4). Gender is performed, according to Butler, and in the performance of our gender we create, across generations and over time, layer upon layer of social activity that eventually becomes so sedimented in our lives that we assume it is a 'natural' phenome-non, which we call sex. The idea of *performativity* is complex, but we can gain some purchase upon it if we consider that Butler derives the term from Derrida – who, in one of the most wonderfully convoluted and bizarre examples of conceptual travel in philosophy, took it from the linguistic philosopher J. L. Austin. The paradigmatic example of how the performance of an act can produce a sense of, or change in, identity is the marriage ceremony, where saying 'I do' changes one from being single to being married. In this sense, 'I do' does not represent something in the world, it creates a change in the world itself; two fewer single people and one more married couple. For Butler, gender is produced and maintained by a constant and innumerable repetition of words and acts that constitute and sustain the link between socially constructed gender roles and claims about biological sexual difference. In a thousand ways every day, it is a matter of us saying, in our words and our deeds, 'I am a man, masculine and male' or 'I am a woman, feminine and female'. For Butler, these are the subtexts of almost everything we do, including the way we dress, the way we walk, the way we relate to others, and so on. Importantly, though, for all that our sex/gender is performative, Butler argues that the nature of gender is not a performance in the usual sense. Traditional understandings of performance imply a performer – an already-formed identity standing outside social discourses – and a choice to perform or not: a choice that must also reside outside a regulative framework. For Butler, the performative re-iteration of gender that produces our sense of ourselves as sexed beings is not something that 'we choose to do or not to do'. In fact, in a further debt to Foucault (who was indebted to Althusser, in this respect), she argues that the relations of discourse and power that structure modern societies *demand* that we order ourselves as either male or female. The nature of this demand is clearest whenever we consider the plight of those who struggle to meet it, for example transvestites, transsexuals, lesbians and gay men. As Butler has argued, listening to the testimony of people who identify themselves as existing outside the sex/gender norm, one is quickly and acutely aware of the oppressive nature of the demand to conform 'to type' as either male/masculine or female/feminine in contemporary political life. If one tries to enact and embody a sex/gender identity that transgresses 'normality' then one's very subjectivity, one's sense of self, is usually at stake.

Butler refers to the basic underlying discursive order that insists on a certain 'normal' repetition of gendered acts as *the heterosexual matrix*: 'under conditions of normative heterosexuality, policing gender is sometimes used as a way of securing heterosexuality' (1999: xii). Butler has in her sights the largely unquestioned assumption that the 'normal' form of human relation is between a man and a woman, and that even if we allow for 'deviant' sexualities to be expressed they must be restrained from challenging that norm – the 'it's all right for people to be gay as long as they keep themselves to themselves' argument, ghettoizes those who are deemed to be outside the confines of a normal sexuality. The effect of gender dichotomy, therefore, is not only to 'naturalize' binary sexual division, but also to uphold heterosexism. For example, Aristotle's unquestioned assumption that men and women must form the basic human association, with procreation as its fundamental aim, lumps together claims about sex/gender with a view to 'normalizing' or 'naturalizing' heterosexuality. Such foundational claims about human nature, if taken as given, can be said to exclude many individuals from the conversation of political philosophy, even before it has started. Butler's work is exemplary in exposing the political nature of such exclusion.

Butler is also aware, though, that discourses and power relations never completely close off the possibilities for change. Given this, how does she envisage a critique of the gender/sex/sexuality triad that serves to construct our identity to such an intimate degree? At the end of *Gender Trouble*, she turns to the politics of parody, and in particular the phenomenon of 'drag'. The presumption is that if our identity as sexed beings is given performatively, then knowingly changing genders may have the effect of de-stabilizing the heterosexual matrix:

> As the effects of a subtle and politically enforced performativity, gender is an 'act', as it were, that is open to splittings, self-parody, self-criticism, and those hyperbolic exhibitions of 'the natural' that, in their very exaggeration, reveal its fundamentally phantasmatic status. (1999: 187)

Butler knows there are problems with this politics of parody, especially that it seems to make gender a (knowing) performance (by a performer) rather than a feature of a performatively engendered discursive regime. Nonetheless, it provides a useful insight into what options may be open to all of us if we wish to challenge the dominance of a two-gender, two-sex, heterosexual model of 'normal' identity. But what implications does this have for political philosophy? Aristotle in drag may be an intriguing theme to pursue! What if we try, with Butler, to imagine how we can philosophize without making problematic and foundational claims about human nature? To do so is to rise to the challenge of difference in political philosophy.

THE CHALLENGE OF DIFFERENCE

One way to consider the challenges raised by prioritizing difference in political philosophy is to take a more in-depth look at the politics of Butler's work, but this time within the context of postmodernism. After some scene-setting remarks on the relationship between feminism and postmodernism, Butler's negotiation of the postmodern and feminism will be considered with a view to clarifying what is at stake in developing difference within political philosophy. For Butler it is a task that is at the heart of political philosophy because political philosophers must always look to analyse and challenge the subtle distributions of power in all areas of life: 'Where are the possibilities of reworking that very matrix of power by which we are constituted, of reconstituting the legacy of that constitution, and of working against each other those processes of regulation that can destabilize existing power regimes?' (1992: 13).

To grasp postmodernism we need a rudimentary grasp of modernism. Modernism (as distinct from 'the modern' and 'modernity'; i.e. as an 'ism') is the justification of knowledge by reference to a grand narrative of human development, progress, rationalization and emancipation. Jean-Francois Lyotard – often credited as a key figure in the formulation of the idea of postmodernism because of his 1984 book *The Postmodern Condition* – defines modernism as 'any science that legitimates itself with reference to a metadiscourse . . . making explicit appeal to some grand narrative, such as the dialectics of Spirit, the hermeneutics of meaning, the emancipation of the rational or working subject or the creation of wealth' (1984: xxiii). Lyotard's main argument is that in the West, and increasingly in the world at large, since about 1945 the social production of knowledge has changed and the appeal to metadiscourses is no longer fundamental to the essential character of knowledge itself. Knowledge was once, according to Lyotard, the preserve of knowledgeable individuals who shaped society; however, the reality of contemporary life is that knowledge has become a commodity available to all. Knowledge has been 'transformed' into information that can be turned into binary code and as such it is no longer the preserve of individuals but diffused throughout society. Although it is a much too recent phenomenon to have been included in Lyotard's analysis, one can think of internet 'wikis' as emblematic of this decentring of knowledge production and transfer. More fundamentally though, as knowledge becomes increasingly commodified in the form of saleable information, the traditional conception of knowledge as that which gives us an adequate representation of the world is losing sway. Instead, knowledge is a commodity that needs governing, regardless of whether it tells us something about reality, so that knowledge itself is brought within the remit of officialdom rather than institutions of learning: witness the growth of political interest in 'the knowledge economy', for example. Given such fundamental shifts in the social production of knowledge, the *postmodern* condition is one in which the idea of an overarching theory of human development, a grand narrative that can serve as a foundation for all knowledge, has been superseded by technological and economic advances which mean knowledge now functions as a commodity in a capitalist marketplace rather than as an end in itself. Interestingly, for Lyotard, this means that the natural sciences have come to dominate postmodern forms of knowledge because according to the scientific model, knowledge can be chopped into 'bits' and 'bytes' which are easily commodified. Underpinning this 'byte-size' view of knowledge are discourses of objectivity and validity that offer ideological justifications of science, which serves the interests of public and private capital.

This essentially socio-economic analysis has been taken up in many different ways, but within philosophy there are those who accept that the old modernist hope of a grand narrative, an ultimate foundation, for knowledge must be given up. This means relinquishing ideas that have been foundational in philosophy since its inception: progress, rational advancement, the increasing autonomy of subjects, an end to history, the ideal of emancipation, the fixity of meaning in the world, the belief that increasing knowledge will free us from arbitrary uses of power, and many more. But if contemporary conditions dictate our abandonment of such foundational philosophical aspirations, what is left? For many postmodernists who accept the diagnosis and have responded with a critique of all modernist and Enlightenment ideals, all that remains is a world of parodic playfulness, pastiche, fragmentation, local but never global struggles, and the reworking of the past but with no belief in the future.

In the light of this account of postmodernism we can understand why some commentators have interpreted Butler's work as postmodernist. She seems to be arguing for the disavowal of a grand narrative that will provide a foundation for feminist politics, culminating in what looks like a postmodern celebration of the politics of parody in the form of 'drag': contesting the 'naturalization' of sex through discursive structures. However, the relationship between feminism and postmodernism is complex, and before we simply label Butler's work a form of postmodern feminism it is worth attempting a thematic overview of feminism and postmodernism in general. As in many other intellectual areas, the 'postmodernism debates' have tended to centre on the question of 'foundations'. In philosophy, the metaphor of 'foundation' is used to signify an unquestionable or unquestioned assumption – or, to put it more positively, a fully justified/verified assumption – that serves to shape the theoretical edifice constructed on it.

In the first instance, it is worth noting that most feminist political philosophy is thoroughly modernist. Most feminists have thought of themselves, and continue to think of themselves, in both theoretical and practical terms as women engaged in an emancipatory and pro- gressive movement: one which sees the task of attaining equality between the sexes as its ultimate goal (think of Okin, MacKinnon and de Beauvoir). This view often relies on the idea that one can define 'woman' so as to construct a narrative of women's potential emancipation from patriarchal oppression. The postmodern feminist critique of modernist feminism amounts to the claim that feminism in its modern variants tends to rest on foundations that are under- theorized, unquestioned, and therefore likely to lead to theoretical and practical problems. For example, the idea of 'woman', as we have seen, may be premised on foundational assumptions that exclude certain women (lesbians, black women, disabled women, women who do not want children, and so on), in which case such an idea can be seen as reinforcing aspects of patriarchal oppression. Furthermore, feminism may assume a grand narrative of progress towards an ideal of emancipation that homogenizes women's experience problemati- cally: not all women may want to be emancipated, or emancipated in the same way. That said, modernist feminism usually accepts that while some aspects of feminist theory and practice have rested on unquestioned and problematic assumptions, effective feminist poli- tics needs a foundational, perhaps 'thin', version of a grand narrative of women's emancipation. Such a foundation could unite feminist struggles, and provide the only possible counter-weight to the oppres- sive nature of patriarchy. A more pointed objection to postmodern feminism is that it is complicit in the patriarchal system by virtue of robbing the women's movement of its critical potential for realizing the freedom and equality of women. So the question that has preoccupied many within feminist political philosophy in recent times is this: does feminism need a foundation in order to be politically and critically effective in the challenge it poses to patriarchy?

Butler is certainly wary of resting the claims of feminism on problematic modernist foundations because she sees these as having implicated feminism in the very structures of oppression that it is trying to oppose. The modernist critique of her work is, therefore, clear: in making 'everything discursive', feminism has no claim to foundations that will enable it to argue the case for the emancipation of women; in denying the foundational nature of sexual difference Butler robs women of the one feature that all women share, a common biology; in prioritizing 'drag' Butler blurs the lines between the feminist movement and other political movements; her politics removes the possibility of fighting for justice for women across the globe because it eschews a universal foundation. The essay 'Contingent foundations' is important, in Butler's *oeuvre*, however, because it represents her attempt to situate her project within these debates by addressing explicitly the question of whether she is necessarily committed to a form of postmodern anti-foundationalism.

In a nutshell, the essay contains three key elements. Firstly, Butler problematizes the relationship between postmodernism and feminism: that is, she takes what many assume can be summarized in a relatively unproblematic way, and makes a new problem out of it. In particular, she outlines the explicitly modernist heritage of the French feminists she uses in her work, and the unquestionably modernist lineage that she draws on by employing Foucault's and Lacan's theoretical frameworks. Secondly, Butler questions whether the founding fathers of postmodernism are really postmodernists; she neatly turns the example of Lyotard into a discussion of how postmodernism is wary of paradigmatic cases. Having made a problem of the relationship itself, Butler goes on to deploy 'postmodern' ideas to question the foundational assumptions of feminism. She unravels assumptions about the masculine subject as 'I', the subject as 'agent', the category of 'women' as the subject of feminism, the materiality of sex, and the goal of emancipation. While this would seem to commit her to the postmodern-feminist cause, Butler then turns her critical gaze on the way postmodernism is presented by its critics. Thirdly, therefore, she questions the relevance of thinking in terms of 'anti-foundationalism', and argues instead that foundations can never be avoided. In an important twist, though, she claims that foundations must be deployed in our critical endeavours with an awareness of the *contingency* that every foundation contains within itself. In this sense, she is distancing her critical perspective from 'strong' postmodernism and trying to occupy a position between foundationalism and anti-foundationalism. Moreover it is only this position, according to Butler, that could possibly engender the real debate that is at the heart of politics, because politics is a series of debates about which contingency matters most in a given context.

The real challenge of difference, then, according to Butler, is to avoid the pitfalls of both strongly foundational claims and strongly anti-foundational claims. The debates about postmodernism and foundationalism intersect with the debates that have preoccupied us since the beginning of this book: power as restrictive vs power as constitutive, universal justice vs the politics of cultural difference, justice vs care, identity vs choice, the nature of the symbolic order, and women's position as 'other' in relation to that order. All these debates require us to take a position on whether or not feminism, and political philosophy in general, must rest on foundations. Butler's answer is that our theories and critical interventions always do rest on foundations, but these foundations are only ever contingent to the critical position we adopt; that is, there is no element of necessity to the underlying claims we make about the nature of women, of humans, of the political itself, or of justice. Butler invites us to consider that what makes politics so interesting is precisely the lack of necessity, because it means we will always have political debates to work through, and political philosophers will never reach a point in their conversations where the nature of politics is finally resolved. Living with difference and contingency may well mean that the norms we employ to govern our social interaction will always be a matter of political decision-making rather than reasonable moral consensus; it may mean, in short, living with the irresolvable demands of politics.

DIFFERENCE IN POLITICAL PHILOSOPHY

The vision described above is invigorating for some, but frustrating for normative political philosophers trying to establish the grounds of reasonable and morally justifiable political consensus. The prospect of having to live with ongoing struggles over contingent truths is troubling, especially for those who want unshakeable foundations on which to resist the claims of anti-democratic political forces. In other words, does the critique of identity in political philosophy leave a hole where morality should be? There is no doubt that this is a deeply contentious issue in contemporary thinking; an issue, moreover, that has occupied much of Butler's work since *Gender Trouble*. In general, and befitting her tendency to problematize rather than resolve issues, she has sought to expose the questionable assumptions that underpin the demand for moral surety (Butler, 2005). Nonetheless she has, of late, developed an ethical dimension in her work that draws from, amongst other sources, Foucault's (1988) analyses of 'technologies of the self'. Whereas moral judgements invoke problematic foundational gestures, it is possible, she argues, to conceive of an ethical relationship to others on the basis of recognizing that one's sense of self is always ultimately unknowable to oneself. Such self-limitation can provide, Butler argues, the basis for a respect for others that does not seek, explicitly or implicitly, to dominate others by claiming to know their perspective. Is this enough to ward off the dangers of tyranny, in the wake of her emphasis on the contingent foundations that engender political activity? This is very much a live issue in the conversation of contemporary political philosophy.

A different approach to the question of foundations was developed by the poststructuralist philosopher Gilles Deleuze (1994) through his investigations into the nature of difference. Michael Hardt (more on him in a moment) has summed up Deleuze well: 'Poststructuralism does critique a certain notion of foundation, but only to affirm another one that is more adequate to its ends. Against a transcendental foundation we find an immanent one; against a given, teleological foundation we find a material open one' (1993: xv). For all the philosophical terminology, the claim is straightforward: rather than set up the argument as between foundationalism and anti-foundationalism – the debate as presented under the umbrella of modernism versus postmodernism – it is better to set it as between two different types of foundation: one closed, one open. Instead of being *against* foundational claims, like Aristotle's, that have conditioned the nature of political philosophy for centuries by prioritizing identity, it may be preferable to argue *for* metaphysical foundations that privilege our experience of difference over the conceptual desire for identity and sameness. With regard to the prospect of 'doing political philosophy differently', the importance of this approach can be easily summed up: rather than assume that we are beings with such-and-such capacities, natures and essences, political philosophers should presume nothing about who we are or what we are capable of. Rather than bring the same preconceived foundational presuppositions to each political issue, the task is to analyse each political situation on its own terms by employing foundational claims which are particular to those terms. Deleuze calls this a form of empiricism, but a transcendental empiricism because the task is to identify the conditions that give rise to a new experience or event (rather than experiences or events which are generally treated as the same). Given this emphasis on difference, the political philosopher cannot come with ready-made concepts to hand. Indeed, a respect for the differences within each experience and event requires a distinctly inventive approach to political philosophy. The task, in short, is to create concepts pertinent to the political event itself: in effect, to draw upon the event to establish the appropriate conceptual framework. In this way, political philosophers will not seek to understand, for instance, the idea of woman by assuming that a woman must be 'the same as' a man or other women. Whatever relationships are constructed, either in the event or in the analysis, they are precisely that – *constructed*; that is, they are not *necessary* to the identity of the individuals in question. But is this really a way of doing political *philosophy*? Is there a danger that it will dissolve into the mere description of particular political events, without any way of linking these together?

In view of the vertigo that often results from climbing the ladder of philosophical abstraction, the metaphysical conundrums this question implies are best left for another time. Suffice to say, one of the more startling attempts to embody a Deleuze-inspired poststructuralist approach to political philosophy can be found in the book *Empire* by Hardt and Negri. The world order, they argue, has changed, and the conceptual tools of an older, imperial age dominated by states competing with each other for resources are no longer relevant. Instead, they suggest, we are witnessing the emergence of a new 'empire', a form of global-political order that seeks to incorporate all identities within it, differentiate people in ways that minimize conflict, and manage people so as to safely maintain the differences under one 'inclusive umbrella'. As empire takes hold, however, its 'other side' is also constituted – Hardt and Negri call it 'the multitude'. The multitude is a conceptual radicalization of Marx's concept of the proletariat; but where Marx envisaged the proletariat as the universal class coming to know itself as such in the revolution against capitalism, Hardt and Negri argue that in a world of empire, where everyone is identified and brought under the administrative umbrella, what remain are singularities acting in common, rather than economic classes. These singularities are groups of people with no real or essential shared identity, but people who are nonetheless brought together by virtue of being outside the logic of identity that underpins empire's growth. The often loose and transitory anti-capitalist movements are held up as examples of 'the multitude' in action.

Putting the old presumptions of sovereign nation-states to one side, Hardt and Negri have opened up a new way of thinking about the global-political order. Of course, one may disagree with them – see, for example, the Passavant and Dean (2003) collection of essays – just as one may challenge any other attempt at conceptual creativity. One general point that can be drawn from their work, however, is that devising new concepts to meet the demands of new situations and events must be fundamental to the activity of political philosophy if it is to meet the demands of a changing world. Thinking back to the opening of this chapter, perhaps Aristotle would have thought differently about men, women and slaves if he had thought to explore the singular nature of individuals who nonetheless 'act in common', rather than assuming that any particular individual's identity is defined purely in terms of their being 'a general type' of person. In that event, Aristotle would not necessarily have assumed that women and slaves are different because they are 'not the same as', and therefore 'not as good as', free men.

The challenge of difference in political philosophy is the challenge of allowing difference into the philosophical houses we build. But, even more than this, it is the challenge of building our philosophical houses on foundations that allow for a variety of houses to be built upon them. Even more radically (or dangerously, depending on your view), it may be that to do political philosophy differently one has to reconceptualize the idea of foundation itself, making the foundation contingent to the philosophical house one is trying to build.

DIFFERENCE AND POLITICAL PHILOSOPHY

All of this 'foundation talk' reminds us that we began this book with a discussion about the nature of 'desert-island' politics (see Chapter 1). It would seem that having built several houses on our desert island, we are now spending a lot of time looking at the ground and wondering whether it is secure enough to take the weight we have placed on it. Indeed one could stop here, leaving our desert islanders to mull over the foundations of their political activity. However, I think it is important to encourage one further push with regard to our understanding of political philosophy. As hinted at in the previous section, the challenge of difference in political philosophy is also the challenge of finding new tools with which to build our philosophical houses, and it is the challenge of building structures other than 'philosophical houses' that may be more appropriate to meeting the demands of difference. Can we think differently about the activity of political philosophy itself and what it may provide? Can we imagine political philosophies which use different tools (which do not, for example, rest on presumptions regarding human nature) and which build new structures (which do not, for example, prioritize justice)? If those engaged in thinking about politics cannot stretch the boundaries of disciplinary practice and language then, it could be argued, those excluded from or even oppressed by traditional – and increasingly specialized and technical – approaches will never find their voice in the conversation of political philosophy. But given the demands of difference, have we reached the limits of the conversational model itself?

According to Habermas, the ideal of communicative interaction is precisely that which enables differences to flourish. A genuinely open conversation, undistorted by money or power, is the basic principle on which all varieties of social integration and democratic politics can be modelled. Not only does a rational exchange of views allow for all perspectives to be aired equally, it also undoubtedly requires that each participant transform their initial presumptions in light of the force of a better argument. However, if we accept Foucault's arguments regarding the constitutive nature of power in shaping our sense of self (see Chapter 3), Gilligan's analyses of the gendered nature of moral evaluation (see Chapter 4), and French feminist concerns about the oppressive nature of the symbolic order (this chapter), then the promise of undistorted communication aimed at a rationally justifiable consensus seems not just unlikely in practice (as Habermas admits), but also impossible in principle. While such issues are too complicated to resolve by fiat, we can nonetheless imagine how political philosophy might continue to develop if we do accept these critiques. What would the conversation of political philosophy look like if we were sceptical of the rational powers of conversation itself?

It is interesting to notice, as one reflects on who is 'in on' the conversation, that the contributions deemed to be of real lasting value, those made by the 'great' political philosophers (ancient, modern and contemporary), are ones that have fundamentally changed dominant habits of thought. Plato railed against the oligarchs and democrats; Locke devised a natural right to private property in order to ward off arguments that sought to justify the divine right of kings; and Foucault urged us to question our sense of 'normality' by creating a new theoretical lexicon to analyse the pernicious effects of this apparently innocent concept. There is, in Nietzsche's words, something 'untimely' about those who have injected new life into the conversation of political philosophy. They stand in an historical tradition, of course, but the novelty and innovation they bring to the conversation is beyond the context that shapes them, and there will always be riches to be found within their texts for 'our age', whatever age that may be. Political philosophy is a conversation but it always is, was and will be a conversation that thrives on new ideas being brought to the table. This is not simply because new ideas respond to new times, though they do, it is more fundamentally because genuinely new ideas embody a critique of identity, of the same old habits of thought, that will always 'speak to' our fundamental desire for difference itself. In this sense, the conversation of political philosophy thrives on difference.

Increasingly, though, it is not enough to note that we can say things differently. Political philosophers are aware that the relationship between identity and difference can be expressed in a variety of ways – through language, but also through the arts, cinema and, not least, through political participation and activism. If we accept that the 'conversation' is broad enough to include such contributions, contributions that J. S. Mill's phrase 'experiments in living' captures as well as any other (see Chapter 2), then we can assume that political philosophy is not just thinking about politics, but also actually doing politics. Or perhaps being involved in politics is doing political philosophy – if one's involvement means challenging political habits and presuppositions, rather than just being a party-political hack strategizing about the next election win, of course. Indeed, if we give this idea room to breathe then we may find a new way of thinking about political philosophy. Though it exists in the textbooks and rarefied journal articles, political philosophy may really be, underneath it all, a mode of engaging with life, and a mode that is political because it involves the creation of new forms of norm-governed social interaction.

Political philosophy, therefore, is not just thought, but also action: or, better yet, it is both thought and action together. Certainly, the norms created through our 'experiments in living' must always be put to the test of normative political theory, but political philosophy itself stretches beyond this because it is the engagement with the world that creates such norms in the first place. As an invitation to political philosophy, then, this book is a guide to orient oneself in the ongoing conversation of the philosophical greats; but – ultimately! – it is an invitation to engage in political life by thinking through and acting on new forms of norm-governed interaction that will bring the challenge of difference to us all.

BIBLIOGRAPHY

Aristotle (1981), *The Politics* (revised edn). London: Penguin.
Ashcraft, R. (1986), *Revolutionary Politics and Locke's Two Treatises of Government*. Princeton: University of Princeton Press.
Bachrach, P. and Baratz, M. (1962), 'Two faces of power', *American Political Science Review*, 56, 947–52.
Barber, B. (1984), *Strong Democracy: Participatory Politics for a New Age*. Berkeley: University of California Press.
Beauvoir, S. de (1972), *The Second Sex*. Harmondsworth: Penguin.
Benhabib, S. (1987), 'The generalised and the concrete other: the Kohlberg-Gilligan controversy and feminist theory', in S. Benhabib and D. Cornell (eds), *Feminism as Critique*. Cambridge: Polity Press.
Bentham, J. (1988), *A Fragment on Government*. Cambridge: Cambridge University Press.
Berlin, I. (1969), *Four Essays on Liberty*. Oxford: Oxford University Press.
Bohman, J. (1996), *Public Deliberation: Pluralism, Complexity and Democracy*. Cambridge MA: MIT Press.
— (1998), 'The coming of age of deliberative democracy', *Journal of Political Philosophy*, 6 (4), 400–25.
Brown, G. (2007), 'Speech to the National Council of Voluntary Organisations on politics', available at: www.number-10.gov.uk/output/page13008. asp.
Burke, E. (1969), *Reflections on the Revolution in France*. Harmondsworth: Penguin.
— (1996), *The Writings and Speeches of Edmund Burke*. Oxford: Clarendon Press.
Butler, J. (1992), 'Contingent foundations: feminism and the question of postmodernism', in J. Butler and J. W. Scott (eds), *Feminists Theorize the Political*. London: Routledge, pp. 3–21.
— (1999), *Gender Trouble: Feminism and the Subversion of Identity* (revised edn). London: Routledge.
— (2005), *Giving an Account of Oneself*. New York: Fordham University Press.
Callinicos, A. (2004), 'Marxism and politics', in Leftwich (ed.), *What is Politics? The Activity and its Study*. Cambridge: Polity Press, pp. 53–66.

Cixous, H. (1981a), 'Sorties', in E. Marks and I. de Courtivron (eds), *New French Feminisms: An Anthology*, London: Harvester Wheatsheaf.

— (1981b), 'The laugh of the medusa', in E. Marks and I. de Courtivron (eds), *New French Feminisms: An Anthology*, London: Harvester Wheatsheaf.

Cohen, G. A. (1978), *Karl Marx's Theory of History: A Defence*. Oxford: Oxford University Press.

Connolly, W. (1991), *Identity/Difference: Democratic Negotiations of Political Paradox*. New York: Cornell University Press.

— (1995), *The Ethos of Pluralization*. Minneapolis: University of Minnesota Press.

Coole, D. (1993), *Women in Political Theory: From Ancient Misogyny to Contemporary Feminism* (second edn). Hemel Hempstead: Harvester Wheatsheaf.

Crick, B. (1964), *In Defence of Politics*. Harmondsworth: Penguin.

Dahl, R. (1961), *Who Governs? Democracy and Power in an American City*. New Haven, CT: Yale University Press.

Deleuze, G. (1994), *Difference and Repetition*. New York: Columbia University Press.

Derrida, J. (1973), *Speech and Phenomena*. Evanston: Northwestern University Press.

— (1974), *Of Grammatology*. New York: Columbia University Press.

— (1978), *Writing and Difference*. Chicago: University of Chicago Press.

Dunn, J. (1969), *The Political Thought of John Locke*. Cambridge: Cambridge University Press.

Feuerbach, L. (1957), *The Essence of Christianity* (abridged). New York: Frederick Unger.

Filmer, R. (1991), *Patriarcha and Other Political Writings*. Cambridge: Cambridge University Press.

Flax, J. (1995), 'Race/gender and the ethics of difference', *Political Theory*, 23 (3), pp. 500–10.

Foucault, M. (1977), *Discipline and Punish: The Birth of the Prison*. Harmondsworth: Penguin.

— (1980), *Power/Knowledge: Selected Interviews and Other Writings, 1972–77*. London: Harvester Wheatsheaf.

— (1988), 'Technologies of the self', in L. H. Martin, H. Gutman and P. H. Hutton (eds), *Technologies of the Self: A Seminar with Michel Foucault*. London: Tavistock.

— (1991), 'Governmentality', in G. Burchell, C. Gordon and P. Miller (eds), *The Foucault Effect: Studies in Governmentality*. London: Harvester Wheatsheaf.

— (2004), *Society Must be Defended: Lectures at the Collège de France, 1975–76*. London: Penguin.

Freeden, M. (1996), *Ideologies and Political Theory: A Conceptual Approach*. Oxford: Clarendon Press.

Fukuyama, F. (1992), *The End of History and the Last Man*. London: Penguin.

Gay, P. (ed.) (1995), *The Freud Reader*. London: Vintage.

Gilligan, C. (1993), *In A Different Voice: Psychological Theory and Women's Development* (second edn), Cambridge, MA: Harvard University Press.

Gray, J. (2000), *Two Faces of Liberalism*. Cambridge: Polity Press.

Guttman, A. (ed.) (1994), *Multiculturalism: Examining the Politics of Recognition*. New Jersey: Princeton University Press.

Habermas, J. (1984), *The Theory of Communicative Action, Volume 1: Reason and the Rationalisation of Society*. Boston: Beacon Press.

— (1987), *The Philosophical Discourse of Modernity*. Oxford: Polity Press.

— (1990), *Moral Consciousness and Communicative Action*. Cambridge: Polity Press.

— (1994), 'Struggles for recognition in the constitutional state', in A. Guttman (ed.), *Multiculturalism: Examining the Politics of Recognition*. New Jersey: Princeton University Press.

— (1996), *Between Facts and Norms: Contributions to a Discourse Theory on Law and Democracy*. Cambridge: Polity Press.

Hampsher-Monk, I. (1992), *A History of Modern Political Thought: Major Political Thinkers from Hobbes to Marx*. Oxford: Blackwell.

Hardt, M. (1993), *Gilles Deleuze: An Apprenticeship in Philosophy*. London: UCL Press.

Hardt, M. and Negri, A. (2000), *Empire*. Cambridge, MA: Harvard University Press.

Hegel, G. W. F. (1967), *Philosophy of Right*. Oxford: Oxford University Press.

— (1971), *Philosophy of Mind. Being Part Three of the Encyclopaedia of the Philosophical Sciences*. Oxford: Oxford University Press.

— (1997), *Phenomenology of Spirit*. Oxford: Oxford University Press.

Hobbes, T. (1985), *Leviathan*. Harmondsworth: Penguin.

Howarth, D. (2008), 'Ethos, agonism and populism: William Connolly and the case for radical democracy', *The British Journal of Politics and International Relations*, 10, (2), 171–193.

Irigaray, L. (1985a), *Speculum of the Other Woman*. New York: Cornell University Press.

— (1985b), *The Sex Which is Not One*. New York: Cornell University Press.

Kristeva, J. (1981), 'Woman can never be defined', in E. Marks and I. de Courtivron (eds), *New French Feminisms: An Anthology*. London: Harvester Wheatsheaf.

— (1986), *The Kristeva Reader*. Oxford: Basil Blackwell.

Kymlicka, W. (1989), *Liberalism, Community and Culture*. Oxford: Clarendon Press.

— (1995), *Multicultural Citizenship: A Liberal Theory of Minority Rights*. Oxford: Clarendon Press.

Lacan, J. (1977), *Ecrits: A Selection*. London: Tavistock Publications.

Laclau, E. and Mouffe, C. (1985), *Hegemony and Socialist Strategy: Towards a Radical Democratic Politics*. London: Verso.

Leftwich, A. (ed.) (2004), *What is Politics? The Activity and its Study*. Cambridge: Polity Press.

Little, A. (2008), *Democratic Piety: Complexity, Conflict and Violence*. Edinburgh: Edinburgh University Press.

Locke, J. (1988), *Two Treatises of Government*. Cambridge: Cambridge University Press.

Lorde, A. (1983), 'The master's tools will never dismantle the master's house', in C. Moraga and G. Anzaldúa, *This Bridge Called My Back: Writings by Radical Women of Color*. New York: Kitchen Table, pp. 98–101.

Lukes, S. (1974), *Power: A Radical View*. Basingstoke: Macmillan.

Lyotard, J-F. (1984), *The Postmodern Condition: A Report on Knowledge*. Manchester: Manchester University Press.

Machiavelli, N. (1981), *The Prince and Other Political Writings*. London: Everyman's Library.

MacKinnon, C. (1989), *Toward a Feminist Theory of the State*. Cambridge, MA: Harvard University Press.

Macpherson, C. B. (1962), *The Political Theory of Possessive Individualism: Hobbes to Locke*. Oxford: Oxford University Press.

McLellan, D. (2000), *Karl Marx: Selected Writings* (second edn). Oxford: Oxford University Press.

Mill, J. S. (1972), *Utilitarianism, On liberty and Considerations on Representative Government*. London: Everyman's Library.

Naess, A. (1989), *Ecology, Community and Lifestyle*. Cambridge: Cambridge University Press.

Nozick, R. (1974), *Anarchy, State and Utopia*. Oxford: Basil Blackwell.

Nussbaum, M. (1999), *Sex and Social Justice*. Oxford: Oxford University Press.

Oakeshott, M. (1991), *Rationalism in Politics and Other Essays*. Indianapolis: Liberty Fund.

Okin, S. M. (1989), *Justice, Gender and the Family*. New York: Basic Books.

— (1994), 'Gender inequality and cultural differences', *Political Theory*, 22 (1), 5–24.

— (1995), 'Response to Jane Flax', *Political Theory*, 23 (3), 511–16.

— (1999), 'Is multiculturalism bad for women?' in J. Cohen, M. Howard and M. Nussbaum (eds), *Is Multiculturalism Bad for Women*. New Jersey: Princeton University Press.

Passavant, P. and Dean, J. (eds) (2003), *The Empire's New Clothes: Reading Hardt and Negri*. London: Routledge.

Plato (1974), *The Republic*. Harmondsworth: Penguin Books.

Popper, K. (1966), *The Open Society and Its Enemies, Volume 1: The Spell of Plato*. London: Routledge and Kegan Paul.

Rancière, J. (1995), *On the Shores of Politics*. London: Verso.

Rancière, J. (1999), *Disagreement: Politics and Philosophy*. London: University of Minnesota Press.

Rawls, J. (1972), *A Theory of Justice*. Oxford: Oxford University Press.

— (1993), *Political Liberalism*. New York: Columbia University Press.

— (2001), *Justice as Fairness: A Restatement*. Cambridge, MA: Harvard University Press.

Rhodes, R. (1996), 'The new governance: governing without government', *Political Studies*, 44 (4), 652–7.

Rousseau, J-J. (1973), *The Social Contract and Discourses*. London: J. M. Dent and Sons.

Sandel, M. (1984), 'The procedural republic and the unencumbered self', *Political Theory*, 12 (1), 81–96.

Taylor, C. (1985), *Philosophy and the Human Sciences: Philosophical Papers* (Volume 2). Cambridge: Cambridge University Press.

— (1994), 'The politics of recognition', in A. Guttman (ed.), *Multiculturalism: Examining the Politics of Recognition*. New Jersey: Princeton University Press.

Tocqueville, A. de (1966), *Democracy in America* (2 vols). New York: Harper and Row.

Waal, Frans de (1982), *Chimpanzee Politics*. London: Jonathan Cape.

Young, I. M. (2000), *Inclusion and Democracy*. Oxford: Oxford University Press.

INDEX

agency 8, 69
alienation 30, 47, 56–7, 70
Althusser, L. 69, 152
anti-essentialism 131–6
Arendt, H. 6
Aristotle 6, 24, 141–2, 153, 159, 161
Ashcraft, R. 38
Austin, J. L. 151
authoritarianism 31, 32–3
authority 12, 51
autonomy 43–4

Bacharach, P. 67–8
Bacon, F. 22, 24
Baratz, M. 67–8
Barber, B. 113
Bauer, B. 57–8
Beckett, S. 147
Benhabib, S. 96
Bentham, J. 84, 108
Berlin, I. 25, 43–4, 78–9, 80
Bohman, J. 114–15, 117–18
bourgeoisie 60, 71, 97, 110
Brown, G. 1–2, 67
Burke, E. 53, 113–14
Butler, J. 3, 149–53, 154–8, 159

Callinicos, A. 15
capitalism 11, 60–1, 110, 132, 160–1
Charles I 39
China 103

Chodorow, N. 93–4
civic republicanism 1, 101
civil society 10, 37, 57, 118
Cixous, H. 142–4, 147–8
Cohen, G. 55
common good, the 5, 42–3, 50
communism 108
communitarianism 6, 97–101
community 1–2, 25, 48, 52, 68, 97–101, 111
conflict 5–6, 8, 9, 26–7, 45
Connolly, W. 120–1
Coole, D. 7
cooperation 5–6, 8, 9
Copernican revolution 22
Crick, B. 5
culture 8, 13, 25

Dahl, R. 67–9
death 28
de Beauvoir, S. 17, 93, 143–4, 145, 156
deconstruction 133, 145
Deleuze, G. 159–60
Derrida, J. 113, 133, 145, 151
Descartes, R. 22, 24
de Tocqueville, A. 39–40, 112
de Waal, F. 4
dialectics 53–5, 59
Diderot 43
Dunn, J. 38